ALSO BY JOEL ACHENBACH

Why Things Are: Answers to Every Essential Question in Life

Why Things Are, Volume II: The Big Picture

Why Things Are and Why Things Aren't:
The Answers to Life's Greatest Mysteries

Captured by Aliens:
The Search for Life and Truth in a Very Large Universe

TRAILING
CAMPAIGN
2000

IT
LOOKS
LIKE
A
PRESIDENT

ONLY SMALLER

JOEL ACHENBACH

SIMON & SCHUSTER
New York   London   Toronto   Sydney   Singapore

SIMON & SCHUSTER
Rockefeller Center
1230 Avenue of the Americas
New York, NY 10020

SIMON & SCHUSTER and colophon are registered trademarks
of Simon & Schuster, Inc.

Designed by Brooke Koven

Manufactured in the United States of America

10   9   8   7   6   5   4   3   2   1

Library of Congress Cataloging-in-Publication Data is available.

ISBN 0-7432-2348-9

Portions of this text were originally published in
The *Washington Post On-Line*

Paris, Isabella, Shane: I love you beyond Pluto
to the edge of the universe and back.
Now eat your broccoli.

CONTENTS

IT LOOKS LIKE
A PRESIDENT
ONLY SMALLER

INTRODUCTION

I have a chad. It is inside an envelope, tacked to the bulletin board in my pod at the *Washington Post*. I recovered the chad from under a table in Plantation, Florida, where the Broward County canvassing board members had been counting ballots (on-the-knees research, the abject groveling for a story, the collection of the debris of breaking news, are skills in which I take great pride). Given the extreme closeness of the presidential election it goes without saying that this chad is potentially historic, and, like the adjacent bulletin board photographs of my children, it has immeasurable sentimental value to me. Bids from readers should start at $500.

We had begun the year fearing that the nation would be crippled by something far more technologically exotic, a software glitch, the Y2K bug, something encoded in every computer and capable of shutting down everything from satellites to toaster ovens. Little did we know that the technological crisis of the millennium would involve a 1960s contraption called the Votomatic. Citizens are supposed to punch a hole in a ballot with a stylus; the ballot design made this as difficult, for some, as piloting the space shuttle. Some voters missed the instruction to "choose only one."

The mechanical process of voting was undermined by its own detritus; the nation learned of the chronic problem known as "chad buildup." The manual counting of ballots caused some partially detached chads to fall off. Republicans, inflamed, swooped in and collected the chads from the floor. This was crime scene evidence. The Republicans asked for surveillance tapes from security cameras in the corners of the ballot-counting room. I kept thinking that it didn't seem quite real, that this couldn't really be happening—the election was supposed to be over. It was late November. We were all out here in what used to be the swamp of South Florida. There is an established way that we select our president, and this wasn't it.

You can't believe how small a chad is until you see one up close. It is so small it has almost no dimensions whatsoever. You can't even pick it up between finger and thumb—you have to lick a finger and dab it. In our materialistic, consumption-driven society this is quite possibly one of the smallest man-made objects anywhere in the Western Hemisphere. It strives to be humble, but seems merely ridiculous. Obviously it is the perfect symbol of the 2000 presidential election, with its absurdly tiny margin of victory and defeat—the great groaning enterprise of national politics and the lofty prize of the White House all coming down to an epistemological conundrum over the meaning of dimpled, pregnant, hanging, and dangling chads.

For the past couple of years I've written an online column, "Rough Draft," a nod to former *Post* publisher Phil Graham's dictum that journalism is the "first rough draft of history." My boss, Mary Hadar, approved the name of the column despite my preference for a name more along the lines of "Today's Incremental Government Process Story." I am permitted to write whatever I want, on any topic, so long as it is produced in the morning for publication on our Web site at lunchtime. In exchange for agreeing to produce three columns a week I insisted on receiving concessions on quality. Two decent columns and one bad column a week strike me as an honorable goal.

The transition to the Internet has not come easy, in part because, when you write for the Internet, you have to produce copy rather than merely talk about producing copy. For years I adhered to a Platonic ideal of journalism in which one did not want to destroy the purity of The Story by reducing it to an actual published text. The Story was a theoretical construct, marbled with hidden meanings, leitmotifs, verbal echoes, and stretches of iambic pentameter that suddenly and deftly give way to trochaic hexameter. Also there would be lots of palindromes.

Obviously I had no choice but to wait for the right moment to write The Story, and that moment never arrived. I was forced to decline all assignments in the meantime. Occasionally a new editor, unaware of my system, would wander over and ask me to "write" something, and I'd have to explain how this was truly impossible, and indeed unthinkable, and that the best I could offer was that I would put the story idea on a list of other assignments I had previously declined.

All that has changed. The *Washington Post* spawned a sister company that runs a vast, deep online enterprise at washingtonpost.com. We are thrilled by this new medium that allows us to give away our journalism for free rather than going through the hassle of charging for it. The big problem is the appetite of the online universe—you must keep feeding the thing, keep filing, regardless of whether you have anything to say. I'm now an appendage of a globe-spanning digital news matrix. I do, for the record, have an editor, Tracy Grant, who, thanks to the wonders of Internet technology, is not allowed to leave her computer even for such emergencies as childbirth.

The Internet is not a medium well suited to those who like to polish their prose and contemplate at leisure the nuances of political discourse. It's a medium for spewing. This is its worst attribute, and, simultaneously, its great virtue. Much of what runs on the Internet is just chatter. Facts are outnumbered by assertions—it's almost talk radio. But there's also some charm in that. The writing on the Net tends to be conversational, honest, direct. Like food, journalism is fresher when it's not heavily processed. There's no time for journalism-by-committee. When online writing is effective, it creates the sense of being at a dinner party with a lot of smart, loud, opinionated people who are still several drinks away from being completely soused.

Some things don't change when you transfer to a different medium. Good journalism has some constants: get it right, be fair, double-check facts, ask yourself if that joke really works, rewrite slop, elide garbage, say what you really think. Don't blather on. Don't steal insights from the smart reporters who sit next to you, unless you credit them. Don't go back into columns you wrote in January and insert sentences like, "I think this race will come down to a few thousand ballots in Florida and may actually wind up in the Supreme Court, where Bush will win by a 5–4 margin." Don't use italics to try to add life to a lame joke when you can get more bang for your buck by leaning on the Caps Lock key.

Consider this book a diary. I've reworked some of the material, cut parts that no longer seemed relevant, but have avoided the temptation to remove the momentary misapprehensions, the truly stupid things that indict the intelligence of the author. Almost all of this was written in a caffeine frenzy on the morning that it was originally published. I have a system: Start writing in my attic around 7:00 A.M., pause to make breakfast and school lunches, write some more, and then, around 9:00 A.M., abandon the column and call Tracy at the office, telling her that I have no ideas and nothing to say and should probably quit writing "Rough Draft" and return to real journalism. Tracy invariably will respond by saying that I can have an extra fifteen minutes to file but no more. I drive to the office, enter my pod, and ask David Von Drehle, the reporter next to me, what I should write. He tells me. I type real fast for two hours and file at noon. Tracy and Mary edit the column, taking out the stuff that will get us sued and destroy the reputation of one of the greatest news organizations on the planet. The column then zooms electronically across the river to the editors at washingtonpost.com. With astonishing speed they review, copy-edit, and format the piece and somehow, through a digital

miracle, publish it on the Web site at 1:00 P.M. By about 1:15 |
I get the first e-mail saying that I am scum, the lowliest slime on
planet, a detestable putrescence. The process has a beautiful, n
ural rhythm, culminating at about 6:00 P.M. when suddenly I ca
remember what I wrote that morning.

This book tracks an amazing year in presidential politics, cu
minating in the madness in Florida. I didn't plan, back in Januar
2000, on writing very many columns about the campaign, but i
became increasingly preoccupying, a good story turning into a
great story, and then finally, after Election Day, into a story for the
ages. Internet journalism is often remarkably free of anything that
could be called "reporting," but old habits die hard, and much of
what follows was typed in hotels and motels around the country.
My editors let me tag along with the *Post*'s legendary team of political reporters; I went to New Hampshire, South Carolina, and
the conventions in Philadelphia and Los Angeles; during the fall I
hit the road in Michigan, Ohio, and Pennsylvania; after the election I wound up in South Florida, trolling for chads. There was no
intention at any point to document comprehensively the events of
2000; these are word-doodles, some marginalia on the historical
record, with much of the material hideously self-reflective, and the
whole mess utterly lacking—now that I look at it more closely—
any mention of the actual issues, policies, important public statements, or key turning points of the contest. It's a miracle there are
any references at all to Bush and Gore.

The reader will note that the material becomes rather less
earnest and more satiric as the text progresses. This was an organic
response to an increasingly bizarre situation. It also reflects a reporter's natural desire, when first covering a story, to be dutiful, to
get all the facts and the inside skinny, to deliver to the reader something that is every bit as much a public service as dependable
sewage treatment. Fortunately this ambition quickly dissipates,
and the reporter can start writing entertaining stories. My own
specially calibrated style is to combine reportage with humor, but

not so much reportage that the product feels like "serious journalism" and not so much humor that the product is actually "funny." It's an exceedingly delicate balance.

One thing didn't change all year: On certain critical matters I never knew what the hell I was talking about. Included in this volume is my confident assertion that Gore would refrain from using a bunch of lawyers to challenge the outcome of the election. On the most important question of the year—who would win?—I offered my own prediction numerous times, never wavering, starting with a column that appeared early in January 2000:

"I think it's obvious that the 2000 campaign is pretty much a done deal, and that Gore and Bush will be the nominees this summer and that Gore will win by 5 to 8 percentage points in the fall."

The point being, never trust what you read on the Internet.

PART ONE

PRIMARIES

WINNOWING
THE FIELD

A presidential candidacy begins roughly five to seven years before the actual election, when the candidate first learns to grovel shamelessly for money and lie without smirking. Three years before the election, approximately, the candidate begins showing up with alarming frequency in remote towns in Iowa and New Hampshire; by this point he will have created a fund-raising organization with a name like the Foundation for Heroic Leadership, or the Boldness Institute. Finally, about one year before the election, and before a single vote has been cast, the candidate will realize that all the talented campaign people are working for someone else, no one is writing him any checks, and his rallies are attended only by people who are being paid to do so. An old, trusted friend will work up the nerve to tell the candidate that his basic problem is that he is "unlikeable." For the first time, he will realize that many interesting things are going to happen to him in his life, but being president of the United States is not one of them.

The 2000 campaign had achieved its essential shape by the time of the Feb. 1 New Hampshire primary. There were two Establishment-backed front-runners, George W. Bush and Al Gore. They had every imaginable advantage: money, name recognition, strategists galore, huge leads in the national polls. Neither, however, had anything like the sparkle of the former Vietnam prisoner of war, Senator John McCain, who was out there blitzing New Hampshire in his bus, the Straight Talk Express. The McCain insurrection was stealing the show; it would dominate the storyline until the spring thaw.

Manchester, New Hampshire
Jan. 27

New Hampshire looks perfect. The roadside snowbanks sprout signs for the presidential candidates—a kind of political vegetation. All the candidates want good "visibility," which means that, even in subzero temperatures, volunteers are ordered to take positions on the sidewalks, wave placards, chant, cheer, sing fight songs, hop up and down, endure frostbite, and die if necessary—whatever it takes to create a sense that a candidate is getting hot. You find yourself wondering what kind of person would be so passionate about Al Gore that he'd stand in the biting cold for two hours holding a large G next to someone with a large O. (And does the person with the O feel just a wee bit jealous of the person who gets to hold the G?)

Here are two guys with pots on their heads: "Pot-heads for Gore." Here are some enviros with a giant inflatable Smokey Bear that, unfortunately, keeps accidentally deflating, collapsing forward in slow motion, until finally the nose touches the pavement—just about the saddest thing you've ever seen. Here are some people wearing jumpsuits and parachutes. Explanation? "We don't want the privatization of Social Security, because it's like throwing young people out of an airplane without a parachute." Ah. *That.*

Of course there's Vermin Supreme, who shows up for every New Hampshire primary, campaigning for mandatory toothbrushing while wearing a rubber boot jammed upside down on his head. He's got the same jokes as four years ago ("All the other candidates are soft on plaque!"), but he's added some sartorial elements, most noticeably a pair of rubber flippers that jut from his shoulder like epaulets. Vermin stubbornly stays in character, possibly because this is who he really is. It's a fascinating performance, but quadrennially is probably as often as you need to see it.

In these last days before the primary one gets the impression that the entire political universe has collapsed around this tiny patch of New England. Everything's pressurized, and there's a strong possibility that someone will squirt out sideways. That seemed to be happening with John McCain yesterday. A reporter riding on the *Straight Talk Express* asked Senator McCain what he'd do if his fifteen-year-old daughter informed him that she was pregnant and didn't want the baby. McCain said that such a situation would be a private family matter. He and his wife would talk to their daughter. "The final decision would be made by Meghan with our advice and counsel," he said. This was a heartfelt, honest, uncalculated, and commonsense answer—but it was also an essentially pro-choice attitude, politically toxic in a Republican primary. Therefore McCain had to spend the rest of the day "clarifying" his position.

He's certainly the most entrancing candidate in either party. The field, overall, isn't that dazzling. Gore and Bush are numbingly on-message, playing the cautious game that front-runners always play. Former Senator Bill Bradley is bland and professorial by nature. Three Republicans, publisher Steve Forbes, radio host Alan Keyes and family values activist Gary Bauer, are quite incredible, in the most literal sense. At this phase of the campaign they are politely tolerated. Long gone from the race, even before the first primary, are such presidential hopefuls as Elizabeth Dole, John Kasich, Orrin Hatch, and, to the sorrow of humorists everywhere, the legendary dim bulb, Dan Quayle.

McCain redeems the field. He's on a commando mission, having parachuted behind enemy (Republican Establishment) lines. He has gone from a blip in the polls to the lead in New Hampshire. Even if he doesn't get the nomination, it's been a historic performance. McCain is not the smoothest or slickest candidate, and sometimes he fights to get his words out, or fumbles a line, but that may actually add to his underdog mystique.

Last night I joined the McCain forces in a Manchester restaurant. The candidates were debating on television, the Republicans first, then the Democrats. McCain's people roared with approval every time their man opened his mouth. He could have said anything, or even grunted, and the crowd would have been thrilled to the marrow. What really rocked the place was whenever McCain got tough. The senator gets tough a lot—he sets his jaw, grits his teeth, and talks like Clint Eastwood. There was one particularly tense moment. Alan Keyes directly attacked McCain for his comments on abortion. For an hour, McCain seethed, offering no rebuttal. McCain has a reputation as a hothead and desperately needed to keep his temper in check. But finally he had to say something. He turned to Keyes, set his jaw, and said, slowly, quietly—furiously—"I've seen enough killing in my life. I know how precious life is. And I don't need a lecture from you." (And we'll settle this outside later.)

After the debate, McCain came to the restaurant. As he approached the building I shook his hand, and for a moment could see what the world looks like to a presidential candidate: You're blinded by TV lights; there are people staring at you, calling your name, reaching out; campaign aides are at your flanks, giving instructions, last-second briefings; there's only one direction in which you're allowed to move. A lane has been cleared. You go forward.

McCain entered the restaurant even as Al Gore's face shined from all the TV screens. Gore and Bradley were debating, having what sounded very much like a schoolyard squabble (they were fussing over which one of them was being "negative"). Someone turned the sound down. Now all you had was a silent Gore, cocking his head a lot and moving his lips, the lack of audio making him seem all the more highly mannered and packaged.

McCain mounted a makeshift stage. The ovation was thunderous.

"Look, my friends," McCain said. "I can beat Al Gore like a drum!"

The place went nuts.

"Tomorrow morning, report to headquarters 0500 hours, full battle gear!"

This was better than politics. This was war.

Jan. 28

The thrill of covering the New Hampshire primary is only slightly marred by the perpetual state of being lost on a dark, lonely road. The typical road here veers randomly through the woods, as though it follows an old Indian trail and the Indian kept changing his mind. The people of this state haven't discovered the concept of the grid system. There's hardly a right turn anywhere, unless you count the interior of Gary Bauer's brain. All the roads seem to be named Route 101-A. It's possible that I've actually spent most of the last thirty-six hours in Massachusetts.

Getting lost is part of the New Hampshire primary tradition. This place is a fun house. The primary is truly a treasure of American political life—a twentieth century invention bequeathed to the twenty-first. Nothing is entirely real anymore in our political system, but this is close. Candidates are forced to do "retail" politics, and not merely as a stunt. They really need to win the votes of ordinary folks with ordinary needs and interests. In a few days that will totally change, and the candidates will switch to large rallies and gimmicky appearances staged for TV coverage, and eventually one of these candidates will actually become—this is the part that's hard to believe—the president, and he will be able to spend all his time with lawyers, suck-ups, and secret agents of the Chinese government.

John McCain held one of his town meetings at a high school in the town of Plaistow. The interior hallways of the school were painted in that institutional green that we all know and despise: a pale, flat, soul-numbing green that has no relation whatsoever to the green found in the vegetable kingdom. The linoleum floor tiles were a random combination of beige, cream, and olive. Someone had placed two large plastic trash barrels to catch the leaks from the ceiling.

The trash barrels weren't there through some political calculus. This wasn't part of the "advance" work, meant to highlight deteriorating school buildings. This was just a real school in a real place. To heighten the authenticity, McCain's bus got lost on the way.

Over in Amherst, George W. Bush had his own gymnasium show. The man has good one-on-one campaigning skills. He knows how to handle a cute baby, specifically an elf named Mollie: Let her play with the fuzzy covers on the boom microphones. "Producer man, you going to put it on CNN?" Bush says to a camera crew. Yes, indeed: Bush and the baby will make the cut of the campaign footage and get beamed around the world. Bush hands the baby back to Dad, says, "Great-lookin' baby you got there," and makes the kind of eye contact that wins campaigns. If the contest comes down to eye contact, Bush is unstoppable.

In his stump speech Bush sounds like a football coach. Not a little bit like a coach: exactly like a coach. It's halftime and he's trying to get his team revved up. He's unsatisfied, but optimistic. This is the speech you give a team that's actually winning the game, but by too few points. We gotta try harder. We need to remember the little people, the players on the bench. We gotta remember the other team is still dangerous. As he speaks, Bush grips the rostrum as though he wants to pick it up and throw it across the room. Suddenly he'll make a karate chop that could do serious damage if it made contact with living flesh. A lack of vigor isn't his problem.

At one point he says, "Listen, I got a battle on my hands in this state . . . I'm running against a good man, named McCain, it's a good contest." This is guy talk, no-nonsense, tough; but it's also Bush's way of saying that Steve Forbes doesn't get to play in his league, that Forbes and Bauer and Alan Keyes are Arena Football material.

Bush begins his speech with a pitch for loving your kids. "You must rededicate yourself to your children. You must tell them you love them, a lot." He talks about tax cuts and the need for a strong military and zero obstacles to free trade, and he doesn't mention the current occupant of the White House, much less anything to do with impeachment or Oval Office shenanigans.

I asked his communications director, Karen Hughes, why Bush doesn't mention Clinton. "Because he's a past chapter in our history," she said.

The blustery style of Bush is in sharp contrast to Gore, who often seems to have just mastered the workings of the tongue and lips and larynx that allow for human speech. It's like he figured it out last night, and today he's going to try speaking for the first time in public. He looks great (and increasingly resembles Ronald Reagan, oddly enough), and he's become a much better campaigner (poor Bradley—not exactly peaking in the final days of the race here—at this point he may be campaigning for president of the Kennedy School of Government). But Gore still has sound problems. He just sounds wrong. He doesn't even chuckle well. The slowness of his delivery comes off as patronizing. What would Gore sound like if he actually *was* being patronizing?

Jan. 29

Plodding, lethargic, aloof, Bill Bradley is nonetheless a hypnotic figure in these final moments before the vote. He's unnaturally serene. No amount of election drama can alter the tone of his voice. Just when you think he has resigned himself to defeat you get a glimmer that he has actually entered some kind of Zen trance, some athlete's trick for blocking out chaos and distractions. Either that or he has been heavily medicated.

His jumbo-size friend Tommy Heinsohn, a former Celtics

player and coach, showed up this weekend to lend his thunderous voice to Bradley's cause, and he put the current situation in basketball terms: "We're coming up to the fourth quarter here. He's taking the last shot. All you can do is take the shot. If you make it, you're the hero. If you miss, you're the potential goat. The fear of failure is not in Bill Bradley's bones."

Bradley certainly shows no fear, or any emotion at all, for that matter. He just glides along. His big strategic move this past week was to go on the attack against Al Gore, but even there he's not exactly letting it rip. He's merely . . . disapproving. He disapproves of "misrepresentations" and "untruths" by Gore. Disapproval isn't an emotion, it's a thought, it's something happening up above the eyebrows. When he demonstrated the other day how he has decided to "throw a little elbow," it looked more like a twitch in his left arm. His speeches are like private briefings; in a packed, oxygen-starved room at the YWCA, with hundreds of supporters ready to rock and roll, Bradley spoke in the same tone he might have used while having a conversation with a friend in a couple of wing chairs by the hearth. He refuses to attack his own party's Establishment; his version of storming the barricades is to pass out leaflets.

The senator has campaign stops that only a Democrat could love. They're a bit shabby around the edges, with no clear rhyme or reason to the candidate's movements, no great salutation at his approach, and little fanfare at his departure. They're too cold or too hot. They're too sparse or too crowded. A Republican candidate would be constitutionally unable to stage a Bradley-style event. Republican events are always mini-coronations. The Great Man has arrived. Trumpets blare. Flags wave. At some point the candidate says, "When I take the oath of office . . ." That's not the Bradley way.

He visited Keene, a lovely old town in the southwest corner of the state. In the town square is a postcard-perfect gazebo and a church with a spectacular white steeple. But where was the town band? Where was the piped-in music? Instead there were a bunch of Bradley supporters buried inside heavy coats and hats, standing in the snow in 8 degree weather, clapping with their mittens on, a sound that goes whump-whump-whump. Everything's muffled in Bradley country.

Bradley supporters don't scream, rant, or rave, but they genuinely like their man.

"He knows who he is. He doesn't have to hire consultants."

"I think he's a man who thinks for himself."

"He's a class guy. A most decent guy."

His next stop was even colder, in the town of Dublin, home of *Yankee* magazine and the *Old Farmer's Almanac*. My *Washington Post* colleague Dan Balz contended that it was the coldest campaign event in recorded history. The gathering took place at sunset in subzero wind-chill conditions. A very modest "bonfire" radiated no discernible heat. On the Bradley campaign, even fire isn't hot.

Bradley spent the first twenty minutes indoors, in some kind of VIP meeting with *Yankee* staffers. Allegedly there was a small press pool with him, but certainly no one piped the sound of the meeting outside to those of us hopping around in the snow.

Finally Bradley came out and made brief remarks. He has his message: We should use our prosperity to create universal health care. We should have a new politics of candor and belief to replace the old politics of spin and poll-driven calculation. He spoke of "moving our collective humanity" a couple of steps forward "to the point where, in Toni Morrison's words, 'race exists but it doesn't matter.' "

Then he went to the fire and ate a roasted marshmallow. He meandered in the crowd. He was in no hurry. Citizens came up and asked questions about nuclear disarmament and the tobacco lobby. Patiently, in his soft voice, he talked about his beliefs—once again, he was in that wing chair by the hearth.

There was no cold, there was no Arctic wind, there were no disheartening polls.

A teenage kid approached. He asked the senator if he'd ever heard of the band Rage Against the Machine. Bradley hadn't. "I like the E Street Band," Bradley said, showing his New Jersey side. He ate two more marshmallows, slowly, with care, making sure not to burn his mouth. If this was for the cameras then there was no sign that anyone had bothered to inform the camera crews.

He may simply have wanted the marshmallows.

I made a point of pausing, every few days, and interviewing an actual citizen, a voter. Over the course of the year I would discover that this was more pleasurable than listening to the candidates. You discover that what the candidates say, and what the news media say the candidates are saying, is not what the ordinary people believe the candidates are saying. What survives the process of repeated translations is the general vibe of a campaign, the spirit. People think that one guy's a straight shooter, one guy's a weenie. That assessment is more important to the end result than any pundit's op-ed rumination.

When trolling for quotes through a town square, it's important to pick out the right people. A good rule to remember is that larger people have stronger opinions. I can't prove the rule empirically but it seems to work in practice. Monstrously huge people can single-handedly anchor an entire story. If you find someone who is actually stuck in a doorway, you're home free. Also, anyone in headgear is good—a hat is essentially a sartorial opinion. Obviously anyone wearing a fez and belonging to a fraternal organization is good for a quote, and over the course of the year I'd learn that nuns were highly reliable.

Feb. 1—Primary Day

The plumber sat at the counter of the diner in Peterborough. His hands were enormous, rough, his fingers the size of bananas. As he ate his food he summarized the field of presidential candidates: "They're all a bunch of thieves. Liars."

I put him down as Undecided.

This has not been a banner year for anger and outrage. If you're really ticked off, fed up, and mad as hell, it's not entirely clear which candidate you should vote for. In prosperous times not many candidates are stumping for the rage vote.

Anger helped fuel the candidacy of Pat Buchanan in the last two elections. This time Buchanan is in a different political orbit, out there among the Reform Party folks, beyond the asteroid belt. Because he's not seeking the Republican nomination he's been completely ignored so far; maybe he'll resurface by summer, when the Reform Party cranks into gear. On the ground in New Hampshire there are still social conservatives aplenty, but this year there just wasn't much indication that armies of people were ready to sign up for the culture war.

Moderation is infecting even the conservative Republicans. George W. Bush campaigns as a "compassionate conservative," and compassion is an emotion very close to being the opposite of anger. John McCain, meanwhile, argues repeatedly, and perhaps unconvincingly, that he's a true conservative. Really, I'm on the right, he tells everyone. And yet the moderates and even the liberals simply adore him. His demand for campaign finance reform strikes a chord with all those who fear that huge corporations and the tycoons that run them have corrupted the democratic process.

McCain's pitch hasn't had the ominous, gloomy element of the most conservative Republicans. He does not warn of the evils that stalk the land. He doesn't claim that liberals and feminists and atheists and Hillary Clinton types are trying to destroy the traditional American family. This former POW can talk tough, but he also cracks jokes and seems to be having a blast. He has refused to become captive to any alleged culture war.

To find a full measure of outrage on the campaign trail you have to turn to the lesser candidates, Gary Bauer, Alan Keyes, and Steve Forbes—none of whom is likely to play much of a role in this campaign after today.

Forbes certainly sounds mad at times. "That tax code is going into the Dumpster. It's an abomination," he says. Abomination is generally considered a harsh word, but everything that comes from Forbes's mouth seems a bit stilted. Rage doesn't seem to come naturally to Forbes, in the same way that you cannot possibly imagine him dancing. If Forbes were to try to dance, an aide would have to rush to his side and say, "No, no, Steve, you have to move more than just the arms."

Bauer gives a passionate stump speech with a Reaganite flavor. "We have been winning elections, but we have been losing the country," he says. "It's okay to burn the American flag, but the kids we've got can't pray in schools. We're losing the country."

Would an angry man find satisfaction with a vote for Bauer? He's such a mild-looking little person. Wrathful folks may not cotton easily to a fellow who has to stand on a box during a debate. (Incidentally, it's always jangling to hear someone like Bauer talk about what will happen in "the Bauer administration." One of the few things we can be certain of is that there is not going to be a Bauer administration. It would sound so much better if he would preface such comments by saying, "In the very unlikely event of a Bauer administration . . ." Or whatever that phrase is that airlines use to describe what will happen in a "water landing.")

Then there's Keyes. He's an African-American seeking the Republican Party nomination in one of the whitest states in the union—a fact that quickly becomes beside the point. Keyes is the great orator of the campaign and can hypnotize an audience. His verbal energy never flags. You could lob questions at Keyes nonstop for seventy-two hours, using tag teams of interrogators, and he would always have an eloquent, impassioned response, never even pausing, as all other politicians must, to insert a little Correct Answer cartridge in his brain. He alone, among all the candidates, has the rhetorical power to stir the latent culture warrior within a listener.

"We had better wake up soon, or we shall fall into the abyss," he warns. (The abyss! How many candidates invoke it anymore?)

Sometimes Keyes will whisper, theatrically. But a moment later his voice will detonate like a bomb, the volume so high that the hairpieces are blasted off the men in the front row.

The Keyes stump speech goes many places, but usually doubles back to abortion.

"Our right to life is God's choice, not our mother's choice—is God's will, not human will!"

He is roaring at this point.

"Without respect for that transcendental will, freedom can be nothing but a curse!"

The listeners leap to their feet as Keyes finishes. For a moment there's not a moderate emotion in the house.

McCain won a smashing victory. Boosted by Independents, he received 49 percent of the vote, to only 31 percent for Bush. The other candidates received so little support they would cease to be factors in the race (though Forbes, with a paltry 13 percent, nonetheless declared the race "wide open" and went charging off to campaign in the politically irrelevant state of Delaware). Bradley, meanwhile, finished a respectable second to Gore, losing by only 5 percentage points. But second was still second. Gore had solid support among Democrats even if the Independents had preferred Bradley. The former New Jersey senator would play on for a number of weeks, but not even a Michael Jordan endorsement could change the inevitable. It would be Gore in the fall. Bush's nomination was no longer in the bag. "Bush's lackluster performance represented the worst defeat suffered by a front-runner of either party in the modern history of the New Hampshire primary," reported the Washington Post. *Conservative pundit Robert Novak said Bush had "lost the confidence of Republicans, shedding the aura of inevitability that had enveloped his quest to be president." Bush needed a win, bad. He'd had every advantage, and now, suddenly, was on the verge of the one of the biggest face-plants in the history of the game.*

Feb. 2

CONFIDENTIAL MEMORANDUM
To: George W. Bush
From: Senior Strategy Team

Sir:
With all due respect, Governor, we need to take bold action to erase the tire tracks running across your back. Right now you're roadkill. We're not advising that anyone panic, or get melodramatic. But frankly John McCain ran over you, then backed up and ran over you again, then left your flattened carcass to be nibbled by vermin.

As your strategists, we remain optimistic that you will still get the nomination. We say this because we believe in you, and because you pay us a tremendous amount of money. But we think we need to take a hard look at what just happened in New Hampshire, and why. What did McCain do that we didn't do? The obvious answer is: He campaigned vigorously and honestly and openly, and told people what he believed. It was a brilliant maneuver on his part and we are kicking ourselves for not having thought of it first.

Our strategy, as you know, has been based on the notion that we can win the nomination without actually campaigning. Our motto was Assume the Position. Governor, we must take off the protective wrappings, get rid of the handlers and the speechwriters, and start getting spontaneous out there. We have prepared a packet of

three-by-five cards containing spontaneous comments that
you may want to make.

Clearly the New Hampshire debacle is a sign that voters
were greatly attracted by McCain's biography, all the war
hero stuff. We need to find a way to match him on that
score. Governor, is there anything interesting that's ever
happened to you that we might highlight? Do you have
any unusual hobbies? What about coin or stamp
collections?

Also you should highlight some of your personal
travails, some dark nights of the soul and so forth. Voters
resonate with suffering. You can talk about that Sammy
Sosa trade! You always mention that, jokingly, as a big
blunder you made as the owner of the Texas Rangers, but
let's repackage that for what it really was, a mistake that
torments you.

We also must reassess the use of your father and mother
in the campaign. President and Mrs. Bush are enormously
popular with a great number of Republicans, but we must
note that *you* are the candidate, not them. Winning the
nomination is different from inheriting it. Also please ask
your mom to stop reminding you to clean your room.

Unfortunately, none of this will likely be sufficient to
reverse the downward course of our campaign. We need
bolder, more direct action. Our strong advice: Go intensely
negative. Attack John McCain where he thinks he's
strongest. Aim right at his war record.

Why did he get shot down over Vietnam? Isn't it time
that McCain had to pay the piper on that? Remind the
voters of how expensive those navy bombers are. Doesn't
it suggest that he's a bit reckless? (Don't worry, no one will
make the mental connection that Poppy dumped his plane
in the Pacific.) You can say that such a thing wouldn't have

happened to you, had you been in Southeast Asia, instead of in Texas with the National Guard.

If nothing else you should strongly hint that, had you been in his situation, you wouldn't have wound up in the Hanoi Hilton. Try this line out there on the stump: I WILL NEVER BE HELD CAPTIVE TO SPECIAL INTERESTS.

Now go get 'em. Believe in yourself. Have faith in your cause. And if you begin to have doubts, if you begin to feel the pangs of despair, dig down deep within your spirit and find that little nugget of truth: You've got more money.

Bush was lucky: The schedule took the Republicans to South Carolina, for a primary on February 19. The race got ugly. The state is so conservative it makes New Hampshire look like Greenwich Village. Bush began hammering McCain on TV and radio. McCain was secretly a liberal, the attacks said. He'd appoint a pro-abortion attorney general. McCain's campaign manager, Michael Murphy, said the attacks would backfire on Bush. "He's losing. He has no message. People know he'll lose to Al Gore. So they're having this negative attack spasm." And yet everywhere I went, I heard the echo of the commercials. People were saying McCain was a liberal, that he had too many friends in the media, that he wasn't a real conservative. It was a reminder, if one was needed, that attack ads actually work.

McCain veered right. "Obviously I don't think abortion should be legal," McCain said. He said Roe v. Wade *should be overturned. He said Vermont's decision to allow gays to marry was "crazy." His claim to be a straight talker lost credibility as he, like Bush, dodged the question of whether the Confederate flag should fly on the state capitol. McCain thought it should come down, but he bit his lip and stayed neutral. McCain would later apologize profusely for his lack of political courage.*

One day, driving along, I saw out of the corner of my eye a Confederate flag . . .

Lancaster, South Carolina
Feb. 11

The Confederate flag is frayed and faded on the pole above Sportsman's, a drinking establishment along Highway 9, not far from the slow and murky waters of the Catawba River.

A sign by the door says Sportsman's is a private club, members and guests only. The exclusivity translates into half a dozen people parked at the bar, drinking beers and smoking cigarettes and cracking jokes. Happy hour has an ornery edge to it. The flag business has everyone rubbed raw. It's all anyone really talks about. They don't talk about Bush and McCain here at Sportsman's. They sure as heck don't talk about something like "campaign finance reform." They're talking about their "heritage." Everyone seems to know exactly what that means.

A dark-haired lady at the end of bar says, laughing, "We're not prejudiced—we hate everybody!"

These white folks don't want the flag coming down from the state capitol. It has become an us-against-them issue. An older lady at the bar starts talking about how wrong it is that the flag may come down, and a younger man, two stools away, turns his head and says, somberly, "It's already on the way out, Ma."

So it's kind of a family affair here at Sportsman's. The younger man is Joe Moore, an auto mechanic. He's thirty-five. He feels like outsiders are dictating to South Carolinians what to do about the Confederate flag.

"This is like what started the Civil War. People come down here and say 'This is what you're going to do; these are the taxes you're going to pay.' The Civil War was started over Northern aggression."

His Ma launches into an example of a local injustice. She has a car down on someone's land, it's private land, in the county, not the city, and yet some government people came along and put a sticker on the car. They put a sticker on the car! Saying it had to be moved or else it would be towed. Apparently the car is not one of the more recent models.

"How do they have the right to come on somebody's land and put a sticker on your car?" she says, consternated.

Her son explains, "That's one thing people do around here. They get attached to things, they may not be worth anything, but they want to keep them."

The conversation keeps drifting back to the flag. The dark-haired lady says, "The NAACP is blackmailing the state of South Carolina."

Noises of agreement all around.

"You read the history books, that flag's got nothin' to do with racism!"

Danny Lanahan, maintenance worker, a stocky fellow in a Miller Genuine Draft cap, says, "They're making it where they're going to take the flag down no matter what the white people want."

As if on cue, a black man pops his head in the door. He needs directions to a local business. Lanahan turns and starts to explain what to do, but realizes it's a complicated matter, and gets down from his bar stool and goes outside to show exactly how it can be done.

It's as though the rebel flag and all it signifies has nothing to do with real life.

There may be presidential candidates running around South Carolina, but they know enough to steer clear of the flag issue. George W. Bush and John McCain won't even express an opinion about it. They have position papers on each and every one of 19,731 other issues—they will happily talk about gay marriage in Vermont, for example—but on this they are silent. This thing's a rabid animal. This is a bobcat foaming at the mouth.

In the parking lot of the Catawba Fish Camp, where Bush had just finished a stump speech, a construction worker, Randy Vincent, who spends his life building roads, said, "If we give 'em that flag, we've lost."

It's a war. Something that should have been resolved forty years ago, or even 140 years ago, bedevils South Carolina in the year 2000.

In downtown Jonesville, a cluster of fellows stood outside the J.R. Dollar Store. Doran Eaves, a white textile worker, said if they take down the flag, they'll go next for the Confederate monuments. Every town has one.

"It's getting divisive in the workplace. I've got black friends, it's coming up, it's turning friends against each other," he says. "I get out of the conversation, because you can't talk to them."

In downtown Lancaster, a few steps from the Nothin' But Gospel music store, textile worker Carol Hopkins, an African-American, had her own take on the flag controversy: "They can put whatever they want up, because I know who I am and that don't make me any less of a person. I got the right to walk the streets like anybody else, and whether they hang a flag, that don't make any difference in my life."

As Bush prepared to get on his campaign bus in Lancaster, a well-groomed man in a suit loitered nearby. It was the former governor, Carroll Campbell. He spent years dealing with the rebel flag, and thought it had all been worked out. Campbell says that there was a deal, to take the flag down and put it in a circle of flags that had once flown over the state. But then, at the last minute, he says, a black legislator from the Charleston area stood up in the capitol and asked that the African National Congress flag be flown as well. And that, said Campbell, ruined the deal. People got riled. The issue became polarized again and the NAACP started a tourism boycott and now everyone's dug in for trench warfare. He's obviously embarrassed.

"It's a throwback! That's exactly what it is!" Campbell said. But he added, "And yet it's heritage."

There's a fine line between protecting your heritage and living in the past. There are places in South Carolina that don't look like they've changed much in half a century. At the same time there are gleaming new factories, immaculate interstate highways, suburbs creeping into places that used to be the sticks. Land prices around Lancaster have gone up so fast that the farmers are getting out of the business. The place is less than forty minutes from Charlotte, there's real money to be made here. But first people have to stop fighting old wars.

South Carolina delivered a huge victory for Bush. The governor received 53 percent of the vote, to 42 percent for McCain. The senator was bitter about the attack ads. He was seething when he spoke to his supporters: "I want the presidency in the best way, not the worst way," he said. "I will never dishonor the nation I love or myself by letting ambition overcome principle, never."

The blow to McCain's hopes was softened three days later when he won primaries in Michigan—where Democrats and Independents were allowed to vote in the Republican contest—and in his home state of Arizona. Journalists were ecstatic that McCain's candidacy still had life. A closer look at the numbers revealed precisely why he now had zero chance of becoming the nominee. This was one of those situations in which my own penetrating insight would be indispensable to the nation.

Feb. 23

The only thing that spoils the drama of the Republican presidential campaign is our knowledge of how it's going to end. We know George W. Bush will get the nomination. Only by pushing this annoying fact to one side, and telling it to "shush," can we plunge with wild abandon into the delicious vat of Jell-O that this campaign has become.

Bush will win the Republican nomination because the Republican nomination is going to be decided by, of all people, Republicans. This is just the way it is. All other scenarios, though arguably entertaining, are a form of make-believe.

I know that comes as a vicious blow to the solar plexus of all those Americans who think that a central tenet of democracy is that anyone should be allowed to determine the Republican nominee—including left-wing radicals, hippies, people who would never allow their child to marry a Republican, members of the ruling Taliban party in Afghanistan, and secret agents based in Beijing. Sorry, that's just not our system. Those folks get to decide only the *Democratic* nominee.

Some readers may point out that McCain leads Bush in the delegate count. Or they might observe that Bush is a spectacularly uninteresting person who has yet to offer any detail about himself or his beliefs that seems as relevant as the size of his bank account and the number of his endorsements. But here's a more relevant fact: Open primaries that allow Independents and Democrats to vote for Republican candidates are a farce. In Michigan, which Bush "lost," he carried the Republican vote 66 percent to 27 percent, according to one exit poll.

Projecting this into the future, using a method called "extrapolation," we can safely conclude that Bush will become the Republican nominee.

The "McCain majority" is a lovely concept, but this is not October. I am under the strong impression that this is still February. (In fact it's going to be February for a long time, what with that extra day tacked on the end. You know the rule: No leap day in years ending in '00 except in years divisible by 400.)

We should also note that it has been an incredibly long time since an Establishment-backed, money-laden front-runner lost his party's nomination during the primaries. Not since Jimmy Carter has a long shot grabbed a major party's nomination. Repeat these words: Walter Mondale. Bob Dole. George W. Bush. None of these men are fantastic campaigners, but they all entered the primary season with abundant money and overwhelming support from party officials and activists. They hit some speed bumps (Gary Hart, Pat Buchanan, John McCain), but their wheels never came off.

Bush will get the nomination and, as noted here previously, lose to Al Gore by 5 to 8 percentage points in November. Believe otherwise if you wish! Don't get me wrong, I'm all in favor of denial as a psychological tactic for getting through the day. The last thing you'd ever want is a clear view of the world and your place within it. No one can stand that kind of pain.

Finally, a philosophical question regarding Bush and McCain: If you could somehow combine the qualities of a pampered, unreflective but essentially competent mainstream politician with the qualities of a heroic, principled, but somewhat bizarre and unpredictable politician, would you wind up with a Great Leader—or just a Crazy Lightweight?

The primary schedule took the candidates to Virginia, which was solid for Bush. McCain adopted a shocking strategy: First he attacked the political "machine" of the state's two most popular Republican officials, Governor James Gilmore and Senator John Warner. Then, in Virginia Beach, he denounced evangelists Pat Robertson and Jerry Falwell as "agents of intolerance." He ended the kamikaze mission by saying, perhaps in jest—he could be hard to read, sometimes—that he was fighting the "forces of evil." McCain's battle plan was encrypted. I did my best to break the code.

Mar. 1

What in the name of Sam Hill is John McCain doing? The one thing we can say with confidence is that he's not trying to win the Republican nomination.

So narrow-minded are the pundits that they have failed to detect this very obvious strategy. They cannot think outside the box, and so they do not understand that, for McCain, *not winning* the

Republican nomination has become a crusade. The man is lying awake at night thinking of new ways to ensure that he'll lose to George W. Bush. His attack on Pat Robertson, Jerry Falwell, Virginia Governor James Gilmore, and the beloved senator John Warner was nothing short of genius. In a single deft stroke, he took a probable defeat in the Virginia primary and made it an absolute certainty.

Let us once again review the hard numbers: In South Carolina, McCain got only about 26 percent of the Republican vote; in Michigan, he got about 26 percent of the Republican vote; in Virginia, he got about 29 percent of the Republican vote. A gift of the human mind is the ability to discern patterns. Here we discern that there is, and has been for many weeks, a very large constituency of voters that do not particularly like McCain, and that constituency is known as "the Republicans."

What's hard to grasp is that McCain has been consciously trying to repel this portion of the citizenry. The punditocracy doesn't want to believe that McCain is intentionally seeking to avoid getting the nomination, because the punditry loves a close contest and is dying to have some excuse to bring out of storage the cherished concept of the Brokered Convention. There are no brokered conventions anymore, but the concept lives on, like the Three Martini Lunch. If McCain had done just slightly better on Tuesday, the talk of a B.C. may have started as early as this Sunday, probably on *This Week* with Sam and Cokie.

But McCain's too smart for everyone. Having likened Robertson and Falwell to Al Sharpton and Louis Farrakhan, he decided to up the ante Tuesday by saying that their influence on the GOP was "evil." What he really wants to say is that their influence is Satanic, but he's too diplomatic.

The obvious next step for McCain is to take on Reagan. For years the party has been beholden to the memory of the Great Communicator. It's a dicey situation, because an attack on the ailing former president might strike some people as monstrous.

McCain has to be extremely careful—he doesn't want people to hate him, he just wants to lose the nomination battle. Perhaps Nancy is the right target.

Beyond that, the McCain strategy becomes harder to predict. What other Sacred Cow is ripe for the skewering? Actually, there's an obvious one sitting in a chair in a big stone memorial down by the Potomac River. Exactly: Lincoln. If there was ever a guy who needed to be cut down a few notches it's Abe.

McCain could go down to the Memorial, point to the words etched in stone on the wall, and say, "Let's take another look, my friends, at this allegedly wonderful Gettysburg Address. Did he really need all those words? What's with all this jazz in the middle part about 'that from these honored dead we take increased devotion to that cause for which they gave the last full measure of devotion' blah blah blah. Hello, is there an editor in the house?"

We now know conclusively that McCain is not a Manchurian Candidate, as some fringe political figures have whispered. When the communists brainwash someone who they hope will eventually become president of the United States, they always insert a very specific instruction about how it is necessary first to win a major party's nomination. That's Brainwashing 101. Give those guys some credit.

No, this has someone else's fingerprints all over it. Let's look at the voters who like McCain. They're people all over the traditional political map. They are liberals and conservatives, they are former draft dodgers and former Vietnam veterans, they're people who are mad as hell and aren't going to take it anymore, and they're people who are just slightly miffed and aren't going to take it anymore. They want change. They want "reform."

Suddenly, don't you feel the hairs stick up on the back of your neck?

Who, you ask, has been strangely missing lately?

Who is the one man who most wants to wreck the two-party system?

Yes, you got it: Ross Perot.

McCain could very well be a Trojan horse for Perot. Look at the facts: Perot has a serious problem running for president again, because his numbers went straight downhill from 1992 to 1996, from 19 percent of the vote to 8.5 percent. He also knows that many intelligent observers think he's slightly crazy, that he seems too much like the hybrid offspring of General Patton and Granny Clampett from *The Beverly Hillbillies*. So Perot has to have a proxy.

The main problem with the theory is that, as David Von Drehle, who sits next to me and is a real reporter, points out, Perot is not likely to feel satisfied with some other human being becoming president, even if it is under the banner of the Reform Party. Which leaves the final, most bone-chilling possibility: McCain *is* Perot, in tremendously heavy makeup. Have they ever been seen together?

Bush won the open primary in Virginia by 9 percentage points, thanks to an eight-to-one advantage among religious fundamentalists. A week later, on Super Tuesday, March 7, the Democrats held 16 primaries and caucuses and the Republicans 13. Gore ran the table and sealed the nomination; Bradley had already prepared to pull out of the race. McCain won a few New England states, but Bush won the big prizes: California, New York, Georgia, Ohio, Missouri, and Maryland. He now had an insurmountable lead. This was a triumphant moment for Gore and Bush; my job, clearly, was to point out their fundamental failings.

Mar. 8

Now comes a fascinating, though fundamentally irrelevant, phase of the presidential campaign, the period in which the major candidates are in rhetorical lockdown and the news media, bored witless, turns its attention to third party freakazoids.

The two major party candidates will have the good sense to

wait out this phase. When they campaign, it will be in the form of photogenic stunts, as they seek to amass footage for commercials that will air in the fall. (Gore already has his Mount Rainier climbing trip in the can.) They'll pose and strut and flex their muscles against colorful backdrops. They'll ride horses and paddle canoes from sea to shining sea, as cameras catch their winning smiles from seven different angles. They'll spend millions renting props, such as huge American flags and winsome children.

At some point each candidate will be choppered to the top of a butte in Monument Valley, just like a sport utility vehicle.

Bush in particular will spend little time giving stump speeches. He may vanish outright. The Border Patrol should be alert to the possibility that he may leave the country. His aides are smart enough to know that Bush is a better candidate when he is not actually seen or heard.

Let's look at some numbers from the *Washington Post*/ABC News poll. In February 1999, Bush had a favorable rating of 51 percent, even though he was not widely known, and 36 percent had no opinion at all. That favorable rating rose steadily. By October 31, it had risen to 69 percent. But then disaster struck: He began actively campaigning.

By February 27, Bush's favorable rating was down to 49 percent, which was only 10 points higher than his unfavorable rating. On TV last night, CNN reported that his favorable rating had eroded to 44 percent. To some extent, this isn't Bush's fault. It's the fault of the news media, which routinely insinuate that the last book Bush read was *Pat the Bunny*. There has been a tendency for reporters to insert dismissive comments about Bush in their stories, with phrases like, "Governor Bush, who is not as smart as this reporter, said yesterday that . . ."

Clearly, Bush needs to get back to the strategy that worked so well last summer, when he never went out in public unless disguised as a woman.

Gore's problem is slightly different. He doesn't gradually turn people off, he does it suddenly. He begins to answer a question on TV and millions of people have the same thought, which is, why does he talk like that and is that something that can be treated non-pharmacologically. People feel they already know Gore, so he has serious staleness problems, plus Clinton fatigue, plus campaign fund-raising fungus.

To cure this problem he has to find a way to allow voters to get to know him much, much better, so that they realize that underneath the incredibly stiff exterior there is a hard but not impenetrable crust, which in turn rests on a thick mantle of aristocratic dutifulness, below which, finally, is a normal person. No voter could possibly drill down to the deep Gore, and he knows it. That's why his strategy will be to bide his time, remaining stiff and uninteresting, and then, at the convention, reveal his inner humanity in a single volcanic explosion. He'll just let it spew.

PART TWO

CONVENTIONS

STREETS OF
PHILADELPHIA

For months, nothing much happened other than the agonizing spectacle of McCain endorsing Bush without using the word "endorse" until prodded to do so by a reporter. Bush assigned Dick Cheney, his father's secretary of defense, to find the best candidate to be Bush's running mate. It became a voyage of self-discovery.

July 24

George W. Bush looks at Dick Cheney and thinks: This is my father's Oldsmobile.

It's safe, reliable, comfortable. Starts right up when you turn the key. Great on cruise control on those long straightaways in Texas. Won't flip over on curves like a sport-ute. Not too sexy, not too fast. The prudent choice.

Dick Cheney! That's a name that is almost as pulse-quickening as "John Danforth." Bush promised, just a few days ago, that his choice of a running mate would have people hopping up and down with excitement. To that end, I've been trying all weekend to catch some of that Dick Cheney Fever. Preliminary results: Feet still planted firmly on the ground. Overpowering desire to nap. I think I'm coming down with a touch of coma.

Cheney's emergence sends a powerful signal about the theoretically possible but, in my opinion, still highly implausible future Bush administration. Dick Cheney is a name that signifies "team player." It signifies "Washington insider." It signifies "generic middle-aged white man." He's got gray hair, a round face, he's fifty-nine years old, he's had three heart attacks—he looks like someone who could do endorsements for lawn fertilizer or weed-eaters.

Why would Bush pick someone with so little sizzle? Obviously it's a safe choice; and he well remembers the fiasco of 1988, when his father picked yappy-dog, eager-beaver, feather-brained Dan Quayle, apparently thinking that Quayle's good looks would prove stirring to women voters (you know how they are—always wanting to vote for a hottie). Cheney is the anti-Quayle. He's all heft and breadth and solidity. Compared to Quayle he's George Washington.

The really tantalizing issue raised by the Cheney news is whether George W. Bush's candidacy is nothing but an attempt to restore his father's administration to power. Dubya is on dangerous ground here. He's got his Dad's name, his Dad's looks, and now he's on the verge of having his Dad's secretary of defense as a running mate.

Next up for George W. Bush: He has to figure out where James A. Baker has been hiding. Pick a job, Jim, and it's all yours!

National security adviser? Brent Scowcroft, come on down!

The Bush clan undoubtedly views the Clinton years as a spasm, an accident, the kind of mistake that can happen in a democracy—a Jesse Ventura sort of thing. Soon, order will be restored. The years 1993–2001 will be listed in official White House literature as the Interregnum. The Bushes will restore decency and probity and high WASP values to a White House that has been grotesquely besmirched by Arkansas opportunists.

Everyone who leaves the White House prematurely—shy of the limit imposed by the Constitution—wants to go back. Jimmy Carter really believed, after he was trounced by Ronald Reagan, that he would someday get voted back into office. The Bush family is now ready to reassume power and, if everything goes right, take another run at that creep Saddam Hussein.

Cheney makes sense as a running mate for Bush. Read the articles on Cheney and what jumps out is the résumé: He was tremendously successful at a young age, chief of staff to President Ford, a congressman, a congressional leader, secretary of defense during the Gulf War, and head of a big oil company. What you don't read much about are his beliefs. That's an asset.

Cheney is one of those Republicans who doesn't seem ideological. This is the tone Bush wants to cultivate. Be conservative, but don't *frighten* people. Don't scare the swing voters. Say you're against abortion if you have to, but don't go around carrying pictures of fetuses.

Some wiseacres might make fun of the way Cheney, assigned the job of finding a vice-presidential candidate, seems to have found himself. But maybe his selection of himself was reached only after much careful analysis of the talent pool.

You can easily imagine that he has spent months checking himself out, digging up any possible dirt from his past that might prove damaging later. He has examined old journals, double-checked the footnotes on his college term papers, and interviewed old girlfriends. He's discovered he's clean. He knew he was searching for someone with, above all, extraordinary self-confidence— and he realized that a man who would pick himself for a job like this was *exactly* the kind of person he was looking for.

I went to Philadelphia to assist 15,000 other journalists in covering the Republican National Convention.

Philadelphia
July 31

Reject immediately this absurd notion that the Republican convention lacks drama. For starters, there's the extremely dramatic ideological cosmetology. The Republicans want to show they are compassionate conservatives, but that means they have to do something with all the folks who are . . . you know . . . uncompassionate conservatives.

These are the people who get teary-eyed as they bear witness to the fact that there is not one liberal bone in their body. If they were to discover a liberal bone they wouldn't even wait to go to the emergency room, they'd just rip it out with their teeth.

These people don't call themselves compassionate conservatives, they just call themselves "conservatives," unmodified, undiluted, unrefined. They are a major portion of the base of the Republican Party, and they're creating a tremendous storage problem this week in Philadelphia. They will have to be warehoused somewhere out of sight of the TV cameras. Newt Gingrich has already been locked in a steamer trunk in the basement of the Marriott. Tom DeLay is under twenty-four hour house arrest, monitored at all times with an electronic ankle bracelet. Pat Robertson has been sent to a dung-covered island in the South Atlantic, where he is surviving on turtle eggs.

Pity Steve Forbes! He has been told that, despite spending tens of millions of dollars campaigning for the nomination, he won't be allowed to give a speech. He can't even wave from the podium! If I'm not mistaken, his slot on the schedule is being filled by Jesse Jackson.

Some journalists are clearly disappointed. Can't somebody get up there and talk about the culture war? What's a Republican convention without a little wedge politics? Whatever happened to people talking about those WELFARE CHEATERS who use the change from their FOOD STAMPS to buy LIQUOR? I'm hoping that at some point the conservatives will revolt. They need a leader. They need Charlton Heston to storm the stage, waving a rifle, shouting, "Let my people go!"

It won't happen. The conservatives are grimly determined to win this election even if it means standing in the corner with fake noses and mustaches.

"The party at heart is a conservative party. It's also more pragmatic," Ken Khachigian said last night at the *Capital Gang* party.

This was a media-intensive gig on the fiftieth floor of a downtown skyscraper. Khachigian is a tenured Republican strategist, a former Nixon speechwriter, one of those guys who has been at every GOP convention since McKinley's. "You know, people want to win. You're seeing ideological conservatism and culturally nonthreatening pragmatism," he said.

Charlie Black, another one of the old-time GOP strategists, told me that only four of the 128 speakers at the notorious Houston convention in 1992 engaged in red-hot right-wing rhetoric. But those four were enough, with Pat Buchanan doing the most damage. "We were upset with Buchanan. He didn't say what he said he would. He threw all that culture war stuff in there without telling us," Black said. "That taught us to be extremely careful. You can't bat .900 in these things. You have to bat a thousand."

Think of the incredible discipline—the repression, even—such a convention requires. The Republicans are trying to take back a White House occupied by a man they think is a monster, a president who was actually *impeached* and nearly removed from office—and yet they can't say anything about it. They are jamming their fists in their mouths. In the privacy of their hotel rooms they make effigies of Hillary, but they don't light up. They just sort of chew on her. Theirs is the hate that dares not speak its name.

Wouldn't you know, the Democrats, who will stoop to anything for a victory, have decided to attack Cheney on, of all things, his voting record. That's how debased our political system has become.

As you've no doubt read many times by now, Cheney voted against Head Start, the Clean Water Act, and Nelson Mandela's release from prison. He's against children and nature. He's against bunny rabbits "on principle." He's against oxygen in the air. He's against certain forms of mirth. He doesn't like it when people break out into song for no good reason. He abhors the salad fork—why isn't one fork good enough for the entire meal?

Cheney has gone on TV to say that some of that stuff is ancient history, it happened back in the 1980s, for gosh sakes, when he was barely forty-five years old.

Aug. 1

Here comes Bob Dole! At a convention devoted to winning, he's the man who knows best what it feels like to lose. He has some theories about why he lost and why George W. Bush is sitting pretty. But first you have to look at him with awe: Dole is amazingly unchanged, an ageless figure, still sporting the perfect tan, still cracking jokes, still speaking in that harsh, flat voice that's like someone pounding a hammer on sheet metal.

He came zipping along a corridor near the Marriott and I immediately ran up and asked if he, too, was a compassionate conservative. Yes indeed, he said. "I've been working on school lunches, food stamps, Medicaid, Medicare, disabled issues for thirty years."

What does he think about the new, sweet, doughy, creme-filled Republican Party that wants so badly to broaden itself?

"We all tried to change the tone and broaden the party," he said. Then he mumbled something about Newt Gingrich—he was greeting admirers as we spoke, and he tends to speak in his special haiku anyway, so I couldn't catch his exact phrase. But what he said next, about George W. Bush, was clear and unambiguous:

"He has three pluses. He doesn't have Buchanan; he doesn't have Clinton; and he doesn't have Newt. Newt was my friend, but his approval rating was 15 percent."

So that's pretty straightforward. Dole feels Newt was an albatross. By "Newt" he probably means not only the specific human being—you know, the guy with the wiglike poof of white hair and the revolutionary rhetoric and the occasional peevishness about his seat assignments on *Air Force One*—but all things Newtish, all the Newtonian physics of the mid-1990s. One almost forgets how brash the conservatives were back then, how they were taking over Washington. Now, in Philadelphia, they're church mice.

Fortunately, there are exceptions.

"Dole was just an idiot. To blame that on Gingrich is preposterous."

That's from Ann Coulter, conservative blond goddess and, with *High Crimes and Misdemeanors*, a best-selling Clinton-basher. She was at the epicenter of the *Human Events* party at the Prime Rib, definitely the place to go to find red-meat Republicans. *Human Events* is "The National Conservative Weekly" and features, on its latest cover, the headline "The Case Against Gore," beneath which is a wonderful picture of a zombified Gore at a dinner table next to Venerable Master Hsing Yun and (as it says in the caption) "Maria Hsia, Convicted Felon." Coulter says the newspaper flies underneath the radar of the mainstream press, which prefers to get its Republican opinions from genial, harmless magazine editor Bill Kristol of *The Weekly Standard*. He's a smart guy, but one who doesn't have the conservative masses behind him.

I asked her what she thought of McCain.

"I used to love him, then I liked him, now I despise him."

Finally, a Republican who's not afraid to toss around a little acid! Coulter said Dole may not have been a true Republican at the core. Being a Republican might have just been a convenience when he decided to run for office.

"The thing I like about Bush is I think he hates liberals. His father and Dole didn't," Coulter said.

Most conservatives here are relentlessly on-message, having spent recent weeks taking extra doses of happy pills and going to special spas where they learned to smile beatifically. They're so well behaved that (and you might want to sit down before reading this) even Bob Barr, the Georgia congressman, declined in an interview to characterize President Clinton as a known felon, criminal mastermind, or accused rapist. "People know where I stand," Barr said, grimly. "I believe that his legacy will not be one that any president who believes in honor and dignity would want to have."

This was at the Marriott, where a gaggle of wingers were attending a reception in honor of Barr and fellow congressional would-be Clinton-indicter Dan Burton. I noticed that in our brief interview Barr didn't even mention Clinton by name—it's as though the president has become like Lord Voldemort, the evil wizard in the Harry Potter books.

Fortunately there's Floyd Brown, the man behind the notorious "Willie Horton" ad in the 1988 campaign. Brown is tall, baby-faced, and all the way right. He had brought boxes of his new biography, *Prince Albert: The Life and Lies of Al Gore.* My superficial review reveals it to be an unfavorable account. Gore and the Gore family sound awful just from the chapter titles, such as "The Sins of the Father" and "A Yankee Liberal in Southern Sheep's Clothing" and "The Eco Freak." The book reveals that Gore was "a very big pot smoker—all that's in there in detail," Brown said.

And what about the Clinton administration?

"It is *the* most corrupt administration in history," he said.

Gary Aldrich was here, too. Aldrich is the former FBI agent who wrote *Unlimited Access,* a best-seller in all the right circles, containing allegations of debauchery, insolence, and Bolshevik sentiments in the West Wing, and the famous assertion that the Clintons were going to allow pornographic ornaments on the White House Christmas tree.

"I saw the ornaments with my own eyes. I *handled* them," Aldrich told me. "Many of the ornaments sent in were foil-wrapped condoms made into mobiles to hang on the tree. Other items included drug paraphernalia, roach clips, hashish pipes. . . . I have offered to sit down and take a lie detector test on it."

But there will be no lie detector test for Gary Aldrich. Because no one cares anymore.

Aug. 2

I wanted to crash the Nancy Reagan reception at the Ritten-house, but found myself swept up in the street protests, carried along in a roving pack of anarchists, socialists, radical progressives, grungy kids who looked like they'd been sleeping on someone's floor for days, aging hipsters, artists, clowns, freaks, flag-burners, and an odd gaggle of kazoo-blaring rabble-rousers wearing large cardboard goat heads. These were definitely people of whom Nancy Reagan would not approve.

The protests began erupting in earnest at three o'clock Tuesday afternoon and never entirely stopped. Center City Philadelphia has become a vast street-theater district. No one has the slightest idea what's going to happen hour to hour, or even minute to minute. It's the Republican convention through a looking glass.

Affinity groups—like the goat-head people—are free to make things up as they go, to change tactics, to form alliances and then break up, to be serious or silly, to get arrested or run away. It must be a nightmare for the infiltrators trying to leak intelligence back to the police officials—these protesters are so crafty they're using the element of surprise on *themselves.*

I first happened upon them at Broad and Spruce, where a couple of dozen people were blocking the intersection. A guy on the ground, Ben Murphy, said, "We believe that democracy has been hijacked by corporate interests." That would be one of the most coherent statements I'd hear all day.

A few feet away stood a man carrying a sign saying "Fasting Against Republican Inaction on Global Warming." This was Chad Kister, and he hadn't eaten in five days. "I'm trying to enact the Kyoto Protocol," he said. I turned to my left and saw an electronic billboard flash the words "Inheritance Must Be Abolished." I'd barely cracked the notebook and already I was coming down with a dizzying case of Message Overload.

Suddenly a protester, standing amid his allies, got news over his cell phone: There was action at 16th and Walnut. They had to go right away. In a pack they raced westward, exhilarated, ready for a confrontation. One protester tripped on the sidewalk and landed hard on the pavement. He didn't get up. His comrades saw him, and one shouted "Medic!" Someone with a medical kit ran to the kid's side. It was like a scene out of *Platoon*.

Two blocks further north they started throwing newspaper boxes and garbage cans into the street. Out of nowhere, plainclothes cops seized two protesters. The take-downs were quick, effective, and unsentimental. One cop grabbed his man in a choke hold and yanked him backward; the other threw his man face-first onto the pavement.

Meanwhile a Hispanic woman, waiting for her bus on the now wrecked street, screamed in rage: "What's wrong with you people? I want to go home!"

She began sobbing uncontrollably. She was a government worker named Cathy Colon, and even on a good day, she told me, her home is a forty-five-minute bus ride away. Her bus had already been rerouted once because of the protests. One wonders if it was any consolation to her that the radicals were protesting on behalf of the ordinary worker like herself.

We continued to meander through the city. It was not hot, but it was lethally humid. I kept thinking of the Nancy Reagan gig— the air-conditioning, the cold beverages, the free food! All those shiny Republicans in snappy clothes. Out here it was Grunge City.

A kid ignited a flag, and shouted, "Burn, baby, burn!" I asked him his name. "Twist Magic," he said. I asked why he burned the flag. "The flag represents a system of control. I am against any system of control." So what would he do if there was no one in charge of society? He said he'd build his own house and grow his own food. (Mental note: He didn't radiate much of a "farmer aesthetic.")

The protesters moved back to the east, then north, then west, then south. The cops cruised around on bicycles with ordinary bike helmets—your friendly neighborhood riot squad.

There were signs everywhere, and graffiti on parked limousines:

"HONK 4 MUMIA"

"AIDS Drugs on Demand"

"END WEALTH"

Two protesters, a man and a woman, were arguing strategy:

"Forty-two opinions together accomplish nothing!" said the woman. Decide on a message and stick to it, she said. She didn't think Mumia—the convicted cop-killer—should have anything to do with the protests. Here they were, protesting the Republican convention, and their message barely mentioned the Republicans. Find a message and focus on it, she said. The man said, "In the 1960s, there was something to focus on."

Finally I headed to the Nancy Reagan event. A superstar TV anchor, an old friend, had mercy and gave me a special lapel pin that allowed me into the gig. Former presidents Ford and Bush, and Mrs. Reagan, had already left, so no one minded that a scruffy character like me had wandered in. I made my way to Bob Smith, the conservative, hulking senator from New Hampshire, and asked him a question that was hot from the streets: Is it true that politicians are in the pockets of big money-sucking corporations?

He reared back, displeased with the query.

"I've been a senator for sixteen years. I've never been in anybody's pocket," he said. He had no sympathy for these protesters. "Why don't they run for office? It's a free country!"

A man named Tom Phillips walked up. Around his neck was the sacred badge identifying him as a Regent. To have a Regent badge is pure gold at this convention. The Regents are the supreme donors to the party—you have to give $250,000, one Regent had told me earlier in the week. Phillips said it was only right that powerful businesspeople have relationships with politicians.

"I believe free enterprise businessmen should have a voice in representing free enterprise for future generations. I started out with a thousand dollars in capital and built a $350 million publishing company."

A few feet away the round of beef oozed hot red juices. On a fresh roll, with a herbed mustard sauce, it tasted perfect. My brain was baked, but I knew this for certain: The outside and the inside are two totally different worlds.

Aug. 3

Michael J. Fox is here, and Muhammad Ali, and it is pleasing to report that Johnny Rotten favors the same hotel bar as the John Wayne impersonator. (Years ago a co-worker mentioned offhand that he sounded like the Duke, and the guy suddenly launched himself on a twenty-five-year Wayne impersonation—a reminder that you need to be really careful about seemingly innocuous remarks to colleagues.)

You get numb to the constant flow of major, minor, and subminor celebrities. That guy two feet away—Joe Piscopo. *The* Joe Piscopo. (Will tell jokes for food.)

And yet as jaded as you might get, sometimes you see someone so shockingly out of place you instinctively do a Scooby Doo double take. Check out that oddly familiar, lanky, slightly shabby figure surrounded by cameras in the corridor just outside the convention hall. Is that . . . could that be . . . Holy Class Action Suits, Batman, it *is* . . . Ralph Nader!

The Republican Party wants to be more inclusive, but this is getting ridiculous.

It turns out Nader had been invited to the convention by a news organization that wanted to observe Nader observing Republicans. He immediately got into heated debates with delegates, raining terror on the profiteers and corporate shills, these stooges for the multinationals, the money-addled supporters of the Big Oil ticket. He was an earnestness bomb.

A delegate interrupted Nader's attack on the oil industry. "Sir," he said to Nader, "there's integrity in those oil rigs." Nader shot back: "Politics shouldn't be marinated in oil. They should be marinated in *people.*"

The situation, with its clashing frames of reference, had the structural requirements of humor ("Ralph Nader walks into a Republican psychiatrist's office . . ."), but he didn't seem to be having very much fun. Nader registers even lower on the mirth meter than Dick Cheney.

The highlight came when Nader tried to enter a VIP room set aside for Republican donors. It wasn't even much of a VIP room, once you looked it over: It was just an alcove off one hallway, a place that normally would sell soda pop and nachos during basketball games. Nader charged the entrance. A young woman, perhaps twenty years old—and possibly completely unaware of the identify of this strange, frowning, scary man—had the job of making sure that only the credentialed, invited VIPs got into the alcove. She wouldn't let Nader advance. He scanned the scene, and quickly discovered a piece of inculpatory information: The corporate sponsor of the VIP room, a sign informed him, was US Airways.

"I'm a *customer* of US Airways," he said emphatically. "I'm a *frequent flyer* of US Airways."

The young woman shook her head: Nader could not enter. She looked alarmed but determined.

Nader, speaking as if to a wayward child, told her, "That's not a good way to treat their frequent flyer customers. Will you feed that back to them?"

And then he marched off, having achieved another noble defeat on behalf of the common man. (The young woman, breathing heavily and trying to compose herself, was a hero to her colleagues.)

Inside the hall, meanwhile, Dick Cheney was giving his speech. The people who planned this convention were strategically brilliant. They knew Cheney was not a particularly gifted speaker—his delivery can sometimes be rather factual, like a CEO giving the quarterly adjusted gross revenue figures—but by the time he took the stage he was facing the most ravenous audience in American political history. They'd been living off rhetorical Cheez Whiz for three days, and here came Cheney, lobbing juicy T-bones from the podium.

Armstrong Williams, the conservative black radio host, was literally jumping up and down, shouting with glee. "I feel like I'm on fire up here! I can't control it and no one can put it out!" Williams said as the whole place exploded in applause.

Just by mentioning Clinton and Gore, Cheney drove the crowd crazy; he didn't even have to say directly that these men are evil demons wishing to establish a world government under the flag of the United Nations. The audience gobbled it up with loud slurping noises, their chins dripping with animal fluids.

Aug. 4

The cynics say the Republican National Convention was entirely scripted, but they ought to look more closely at the facts.

Several parties ran out of grilled salmon prematurely. At the lavish "IRA-Palooza" party, sponsored by American Express, Merrill Lynch, Morgan Stanley Dean Witter, and a few other mom-and-pop operations, the crab cake mini-sandwiches registered on my palate as dry. Things were getting mighty primitive out there, it was practically a Lord of the Flies situation. I could see the anguish on the faces of some of the Republicans—that unmistakable look that says, "Lord, I beseech Thee to refresh my beverage."

There was one guy at IRA-Palooza who was actually taking the crab cake patties off their little buns, and tossing the buns back into the pile. He was a crabmeat raider, a separatist, someone who just wants the good part, the kind of guy who eats only the creme filling of the Oreo. That's the Republicans for you! When the Democrats have their gluttonous corporate-bought soirees in Los Angeles they're going to eat the crabmeat *and* the bun and maybe stuff a few shrimps in there in one great egalitarian wad of food.

SO MANY MEMORIES.

We will remember when George W. Bush took the stage and, within sixty seconds, compared himself to George Washington. We will remember his excellent posture, his firm resolve, and his many fine lines stolen directly from Ted Kennedy. We will remember that someone miscalculated the amount of balloons and confetti that would be necessary at the end, and how the candidate and his wife totally disappeared in a blizzard of red, white, and blue.

We will remember the night we saw the first nationally televised speech of twenty-four-year-old, movie-star-handsome George P. Bush, our future president.

We will remember that throughout the convention the Republican Party highlighted the fact that it has literally dozens of black and Latino members, each of whom spoke in prime time.

What I'll remember most, and forgive me if this seems weird, is the Mutter Museum, with its wall of human skulls and a corpse that had turned to soap. I didn't intend to go, but it turned out that the museum, a collection of medical abnormalities at the College of Physicians, was just downstairs from the *National Review* party in honor of presidential impeacher Henry Hyde. I do not stoop to the easy analogy and thus will not seek to find "humor" in a comparison of conservative Republicans and a museum's collection of repulsive anatomic oddities. That's the kind of har-har, nyuk-nyuk move you get in a Bill Safire column, but not here.

I will note, however, that Ralph Reed's use of the phrase "bold reform agenda" when I asked him about the convention—followed seconds later by another mention of the "bold reform agenda," then, quickly, a third mention of the "bold reform agenda," all in a span of about fifteen seconds—did seem every bit as mind-boggling as the exhibit downstairs of a lady with a ten-inch horn jutting from her forehead.

And don't even talk to me about the giant human bowel! That's beyond the pale, and the only thing I'll say is that this thing is quite literally the size of a duffel bag. It would probably be too big for carry-on luggage. This was the result of a historic case of constipation, the exhibit stated, "which terminated fatally in the adult." It was probably from all those cheesesteaks.

We'll all remember, vaguely, as if in a haze, the image of street protesters showing their displeasure with corporate America by knocking trash cans into the street and running away really fast. We will shake our heads in awe at the realization that they made the Philadelphia Police Department look gentle. This is the most astonishing turn of events since *Big Brother* came on the air and made *Survivor* look like a Ken Burns series. The protesters are, in most every case, sincere and committed, but they might want to consider switching their strategy toward one that is designed to make people *agree* with them.

We will all remember the drama of John McCain, who grimaced his way through a speech in which he did not once mention the words "campaign finance reform." Where do we find such men?

I will remember riding a golf cart around the convention center with, of all people, Frank Rizzo, son of the take-no-prisoners former mayor and police commissioner with the same name. The elder Rizzo, according to the *Philadelphia Inquirer,* once went to the scene of a riot and waved a nightstick, shouting, "Go ahead, men! Get their asses!" But that was the old Philly. The younger Rizzo, a city councilman, has seen his city get cleaned up, has seen first-class restaurants open throughout the downtown. Now he was bearing witness to the spectacle of a full-bore national media event, with acres of satellite dishes, thousands of landlines, fifteen thousand journalists, excess piled on excess. What'd he think of all this?

"It's beyond . . ."

He paused.

"It's beyond Superman," he said.

Exactly right. These things are way, way beyond Superman. They're vintage Americana. The only thing that could make the political conventions even more spectacular, more amazing, more wondrous, would be actual news.

DEEP INTO
HOLLYWOOD

The political conventions of 2000 were supposed to be coming-out parties for all the various Internet news operations. Never before had any event been so maximally wired for online coverage. We were ready to cover World War III. The audience, however, declined to materialize in the expected numbers. Word went around that the Internet coverage was a bust. Technological brute force could not by itself create an "Internet story."

Bush, meanwhile, had surged far ahead, up 18 points in one poll. The Democrats would need a bounce from their convention in Los Angeles. Gore had become an oddly indistinct figure on the political landscape, barely remembered. President and Mrs. Clinton weren't helping matters, as they planned to arrive early in Los Angeles to attend glittery fund-raisers for Hillary's Senate campaign. They also had commandeered pretty much the entirety of the first night of the convention. They were stealing the show and, not incidentally, a lot of the money that might have gone to the party nominee—what's-his-face.

Less than a week before the convention, Gore made a bold move: He picked as his running mate a man who was most famous for making a speech denouncing President Clinton's behavior in the Lewinsky matter. It was a delicious moment for armchair psychologists. The Beta Male was finally making his move against the Alpha. Pundits went into a frenzy; I did my best, on deadline, to pound out something that was certain to be unduplicated by any other political observer.

Aug. 11

This just in: The Democrats are playing the Lewinsky card. It's bizarre. It's counterintuitive. It could turn out brilliantly. I believe it is part of the Deep Game, an ultrasecret strategy that is three or four levels of strategy below the surface strategy.

Consider a few facts. The Republicans in Philadelphia managed to get through the entire week without directly speaking about Oval Office gropings, the impeachment, the blue dress, or anything of the sort. At one point George W. Bush mentioned the word "scandal," but he did it so quickly it barely registered. Instead, the Republicans spoke in code, saying they would restore "honor" and "dignity" to the nation's highest office, without adding that they would have the whole place "steam-cleaned" and "thoroughly disinfected."

The Democrats, watching and listening, saw an opening. If the Republicans weren't going to exploit to its fullest extent the Lewinsky scandal, the Democrats would. Cut to this week. The vice president has a choice of sensible running mates, but he surprises everyone by picking the one who is by far the most moralistic. The whole "Jewish" issue is just cover. Joe Lieberman gets picked because he dreams at night of passing new laws against jaywalking. He's sanctimony incarnate.

The tactic works beautifully: The news media gleefully resurrect Lieberman's 1998 speech calling Clinton's actions "immoral." The electorate is forced to remember a trauma that has been carefully repressed. Long-dormant neurons start firing Starr Report footnotes from one hemisphere of the brain to the other.

But the Democrats aren't done. They must pound home the notion that they are vulnerable on moral issues. Thus they concoct an entirely new sex-related controversy, this time about a fund-raiser being thrown at the Playboy Mansion by Representative Loretta Sanchez. The party bosses say they're horrified by the association with a sleaze peddler like Hugh Hefner.

All this is staged for maximum media sensationalism. Unless Sanchez moves the party, the result will be massive, almost round-the-clock coverage of the alliance between the Democratic Party and the flesh industry.

A strategic blunder? Not at all. The Democrats want to bring up moral issues because they want to remind everyone of the Lewinsky scandal—all in keeping with a theory that the American people blame the Republicans for the scandal more than they blame President Clinton. His were sins of a base nature; the Republicans, however, carefully considered and carried out their prosecution of the president. Blame for the national nightmare is thus meted out according to the extent to which the sin is premeditated.

The designers of the Deep Game know they need still another bold move if they want to implement fully their strategy of victory-through-self-abasement. So guess what they do: They sacrifice the king himself. They tell President Clinton he must once again confess his profound remorse for mistakes that the entire country no longer wants to think about.

The president dutifully goes to a meeting of evangelists in suburban Chicago for a very public encounter session. The president says, "I'm now in the second year of a process of trying to totally rebuild my life from a terrible mistake I made."

He doesn't proclaim triumph. He doesn't say he has conquered his reptilian urges. Instead, he says, "It's always a work in progress and you just have to hope that you're getting better every day, but if you're not getting better, chances are you're getting worse; that, you know, this has to be a dynamic, ongoing effort."

In other words, he's raising the specter of relapse. He's saying, I'm holding it together, but any second now I could be at Hef's, swimming in his grotto.

The Deep Game is unfolding so fast, even the professional pundits are dazed. The triple-backloop subterranean Democratic strategy is so complicated you can't measure the results with a poll.

No one can quite see how any of this plays to the advantage of Al Gore—which, again, is exactly what makes the strategy so inspired.

I don't think we should even be sure that Al Gore actually wants to win the election. "Winning" is just a surface strategy. Gore may have bigger fish to fry. He may represent people for whom a Gore loss is preferable to a Gore victory.

Remember: The people who run this thing are completely unknown to us, and it's only when we think we've finally figured out their motives that we've arrived at the point where we've been completely snookered.

Los Angeles
Aug. 14

There's not much that's democratic about the Democratic National Convention. It appears that the priority for party leaders this week is to hobnob with Hollywood moguls and movie stars. There is a dazzling array of parties to which you, the ordinary person, are specifically not invited. Some parties, like David Geffen's, or Barbra Streisand's, are so exclusive you have to be on a special list even to be allowed to think about them. Forget I brought it up.

The convention itself doesn't entirely radiate a sense of a happy democracy, what with the imposing security fence surrounding the entirety of the convention center complex. It looks like an industrial prison fence, anchored in concrete, bent outward at the top to make an exterior assault all the more difficult. In a concession to democracy it is not topped by barbed wire. It's possible that the Democrats, looking carefully at poll numbers, are hoping to keep Al Gore from getting inside.

Through journalistic connections I managed to get on a special list that allowed me to stand in the broiling heat outside Studio 23 on the Warner Brothers lot, where I was able to watch people whose names were on an even more special list attend a party on the set of the TV show *The West Wing*. I was covering what is known as "arrivals."

When you cover "arrivals" your job is to watch the famous, important, powerful people—the people who are "players"—arriving at the party. You have to hope they'll stop and talk for a moment as they stroll up the red carpet and snag flutes of champagne from silver trays held by waiters in black tie. I was separated from the party guests by a velvet rope. The Warner Brothers publicity people did provide those of us on the outside with bottled water and sodas. Although they later rejected my request for one of the goodie bags, they were still perfectly pleasant about it.

So the whole thing was fairly civilized, as intensely humiliating things go.

It was hot. It was, indeed, scorching. But heat is democratic. Sweating is democratic. When you stand in the heat in the media scrum, covering "arrivals," you feel democratic down to your pores.

Martin Sheen arrived. He plays President Josiah Bartlet. So debased has my station in life become that, instead of telling him how much I liked *Badlands,* or asking him to reenact the mirror-punching scene in *Apocalypse Now,* I asked him a bunch of substantive questions about politics. (True fact: At these convention parties you feel like a phony, a completely artificial person, if you talk about serious political issues. The other party-goers will play along, but you can tell they pity you, because you just don't get it.)

Have the Democrats become too beholden to corporate interests?

"I think all of us are in danger of surrendering too much to corporate America," Sheen answered. "I would wish that the party would be more liberal, of course. I'm an old Democrat. I'm a Kennedy Democrat."

Jack Valenti, legendary lobbyist for the film industry, arrived to lusty greetings ("My hero!" proclaimed Gerald Levin, head of Time Warner and the boss of everything in sight). Valenti is Hollywood in human form, magnificently tan, handsome, with a comb within easy reach for an emergency spin through his shock of white hair. In keeping with his job as a representative of the industry, he is a small man with a large head.

He rejected any suggestion that Hollywood is at fault for generating trashy movies.

"Hollywood is not a monolith," he said. There were 660 movies produced last year, he said, and no one can tell the makers of all those movies what to do. Besides, crime is down in America. If violent movies cause crime, he said, and there are more violent movies, then how come crime has fallen?

"What about the Internet? You can go on the Internet and see unbelievable stuff!" he said. "It's squalid!"

Those of us from Washington were interested in the Hollywood stars who were arriving; the Hollywood media people were interested in the real White House staffers who were here to mingle with their television counterparts. What's confusing is that, in Los Angeles, even nobodies sometimes look like celebrities. You can't tell if that guy over there with the nice suit and the slicked-back hair is a celebrity or just one of the Warner Brothers security guards—or, more confusingly, if he's an actor who plays a security guard on the TV show.

Donna Shalala, secretary of health and human services, came along, and ventured that there's nothing wrong with the schmoozy relationship between the Democrats and Hollywood.

"This is part of our convention. And politics *is* glitzier. We use glitz to communicate our messages," she said. "We've learned a lot from Hollywood about how to communicate."

The party started to wind down. One of the guests, leaving, complained that she couldn't get into the Oval Office portion of the TV set. The Oval Office wasn't like the rest of the set. To get in, you had to be wearing a special pin. And how did you get the special pin?

"You had to be on a special-pin list."

Aug. 15

The Clintons were about to speak inside the Staples Center when, just outside, the very loud band Rage Against the Machine got several thousand people jumping up and down in a warm-up exercise for the rioting to come later. Rage Against the Machine is not a subtle band, and the musicians play their instruments as though they want to destroy them. My impression was that the band members are not Gore Democrats. The tip-off may have been the moment the band led the crowd in a chant of "F—k Gore! F—k Gore!"

But at least Gore got mentioned. The vice president has had the feeblest of profiles at what has been, so far, Clinton Convention III.

Speakers cite Gore's name dutifully, but he needs to get into town quickly, in some dramatic way, perhaps landing in a parachute or descending in a one-man helicopter. He should show up with green hair or with a pierced nose, or with his Secret Brother, or with a radically intensified Southern accent and a wad of Red Man in his cheek. What Al Gore can't do at this point is be Al Gore. That's courting catastrophe.

President Clinton has completely stolen the show, starting with his rockstar entrance into the Staples Center, a Long March through the backstage corridors, alone, chin up, a single camera documenting his journey. As he neared the stage the audience roared, cheered, and squealed. To my limited knowledge it was the most egregiously self-aggrandizing and pretentious moment in the history of the presidency. Some of us in the press corps were hoping he'd have a Spinal Tap misadventure, get lost back there in the bowels of the arena, and finally burst through some security doors into the parking lot.

What the convention really needs is more split-screen coverage. Just as the president was speaking, the police were taking action outside, clearing the protest area by force. A police spokesman told me earlier in the day that the police want to "facilitate" the protests. He said, "We're all prepared to facilitate the two-thirty march and the five o'clock march." From what I could see later on TV, they might want to use fewer rubber bullets in their facilitation.

As in Philadelphia, the protests are chaotic and all over the place, geographically and ideologically. You got your anti–death penalty folks, your anarchists, your socialists, and your people with extremely specific issues, carrying signs saying "Gore-Oxy Out of U'Wa Land" or "Save Ballona Wetlands." One man wore a fake nose and mustache, and carried a "Vote Lemming" sign. I'm not sure who was behind the disguise, but he vaguely resembled Michael Dukakis.

By definition, conventions are about crowds, about flesh converging, about thousands of people finding themselves sucked into some central mosh pit of political togetherness. You can't come to a convention if you have an aversion to physical contact. The whole point of the thing is to create a throng, to literally rub elbows. You hear speeches, you eat and drink, but the main thing you do is search for the center of gravity.

The mosh pit inside, on the convention floor, features famous TV correspondents and anchorpersons mixing it up with senators and cabinet officers and, almost as an afterthought, the delegates. Everyone has to keep moving. If people stop moving the place will congeal into a hardened mass of meat.

The central tenet of the Democratic Party has always been "More." More government. Longer speeches. Physically bigger delegates. You walk through the convention hall, you'll see some mighty well-fed Democrats. You get the sense that this is not a party that's terribly adept at dieting. There are also simply more delegates than at a Republican convention. The Democrats have determined that they cannot nominate a candidate unless they have the participation of 4,300 delegates. There are 270 from a single government workers union, AFSCME.

The Democrats also throw parties with more guests than the Republicans—about twelve thousand people, in the case of California Governor Gray Davis's party at the Paramount backlot Monday night. This was an eight-searchlight party. At the entrance was a roller coaster, a series of long, phallic balloons that streamed toward the night sky, some Hawaiian dancers, a Jim Carrey impersonator, a faux Joan Rivers, and, dangerously, a slinky Marilyn Monroe, perhaps hoping to sing "Happy Birthday" to the president.

By Hollywood standards, the party was a bit too democratic. It was so democratic there were actual *delegates* in attendance. That's always a red flag, a sign of a shindig in serious trouble. Delegates wear funny hats and buttons and are true believers with a sense of purpose. They play important roles in their communities and work as teachers and nurses and union organizers. They are decent, hardworking, fair people. That's not the element you want at a Hollywood party.

"This is the kind of party I like. Fanfare!" said Virginia Graves, a delegate from Salisbury, North Carolina.

"Fanfare. Action. Hopefully food," said her friend, Shirley Wiggins of Gastonia, North Carolina.

So you see the problem. These bad apples show up, looking for fanfare, and you find yourself scanning the crowd, wondering, where are the vain, loutish egomaniacs? You want billionaires. You want TV talk show screamers. You want movie stars with giant heads and a steady stream of emaciated starlets. It was looking pretty grim until Angelica Huston showed up. I asked her what she thought of Gore. She said what everyone had been thinking: "He's got a tough act to follow."

Aug. 16

Security is so tight here that merely exiting the convention and entering the streets of downtown Los Angeles can be an ordeal. You have to hike across the vast parking lots and find one of the narrow gates in the infamous fence that surrounds the complex. Last night the queue to leave stretched as long as a football field, and for a moment I feared that the police were now requiring a special credential to enter the outside world—or, worse, an engraved invitation. "I'm sorry, you're not on the list," they might say, forcing me to turn around and spend the night on the floor of the Staples Center.

Only when I finally punched through the perimeter did the reason for the delay become clear. When you exit the compound, you have to run the Causes Gauntlet.

"Al Gore supports sweatshops!"

"Go ahead, vote for genocide!"

"No blood for oil; end the sanctions now!"

"Corporate tools! Corporate tools!"

The people with the causes lined both sides of the sidewalk. A man in a ragged robe held an enormous cross. Another held a photograph of an aborted fetus. A third had a sign saying "Romans Go Home. Welcome Visigoths."

So it's a diverse coalition. One consistent theme is the revulsion at corporate America and the consumer culture it has spawned. The more radical protesters believe they are trapped in a police state. Imagine how validated they must feel, getting shot with rubber bullets in downtown Los Angeles outside a convention ringed with a prison-caliber fence.

Last night, the cops busted fifty people for riding bicycles. These weren't exactly the Hell's Angels. Their radical cause includes a demand for more bike lanes. They're linked to a San Francisco–based group called Critical Mass, which wants to take back the streets from the car culture.

I stumbled across the big bicyclist bust while walking to Arianna Huffington's Shadow Convention. Sympathetic witnesses said the cyclists were forced, by police barriers, to ride the wrong way down a one-way street, which triggered a sudden crackdown. "The response has been totally out of proportion to the thing itself. It's as though this was a terrorist attack," said one witness, Cherilyn Parsons.

The captured cyclists were handcuffed in a line along a chain link fence on Flower Street, directly under an off-ramp for the I-10 overpass. They were not allowed to move. More than a hundred police officers stood in rigid formation along the street. A few carried heavy weapons, including one that looked like it would be handy for launching grenades.

"Shame! Shame!" shouted the protesters.

A young guy eating an apple, one of the bikers who escaped, surveyed the scene without the slightest trace of rage. He was slowly, deliberately eating his apple down to the core, seeds and all. I was struck by his calm demeanor. "This is a police state—and here's the proof," he said.

He had his confirmation; perhaps there's serenity in that.

Los Angeles is a strange land, one of the strangest. The future of America is already here. There are sharp divisions between rich and poor. There are millions of immigrants. There are gangs, riots, street violence. There is bad air and not enough water. The traffic jams are apocalyptic.

Sometimes the great issues of our day can sound rather abstract, especially when spoken on a stage. To make them come alive, you just need to leave the building and go for a walk—if that's still allowed.

Aug. 17

We heard last night from his adorable daughter, Karenna Gore Schiff, and from his craggy-faced college buddy, Tommy Lee Jones. The message: Al Gore, despite all appearances, is an actual human being. He's super nice. He does normal-person things all the time. He's only weirdly stiff, mannered, and mechanical on the exterior. You'd really like him if you were to spend twenty or twenty-five years getting to know him.

"He's been the most wonderful father in the whole world," said the adorable daughter.

"He is a good, caring, loving man," said the craggy-faced college buddy.

They painted charming vignettes. Al Gore shooting pool. Al Gore running with the coon dogs through the Tennessee woods. Al Gore slathering butter on the toast in the morning. He helped with the dinosaur diorama! When the kids camped in the backyard igloo, he brought them hot chocolate and warm blankets! What a mensch.

Gore has no choice but to put this stuff out there, because after eight years as vice president, and a quarter century in elected office, he still hasn't succeeded in convincing a majority of Americans that he's likable. A startling poll in *USA Today* showed that 47 percent of likely voters say there's "no chance whatsoever" they'd ever vote for him. The Gore people have to pray that part of the problem is that Gore still—still!—hasn't sufficiently introduced himself.

His problem is partly what has been called the High Southern Formal speaking style. It's incorrect to say that Gore speaks down to people, as though they're children. Rather, he speaks as though he's addressing his grandmother in her parlor.

His father spoke in that same tone to his son throughout the lad's childhood. The princeling was to the manor born. Combine that with a tendency toward political caution (a little voice in his head is constantly screaming Danger! Danger!) and you have something that is the opposite of combustible. I think one scientific term that's applicable is "vitrification."

So what we saw last night wasn't the nomination of Al Gore so much as the attempted humanization. As we await his big speech tonight, we have to wonder how far he'll go in his campaign to seem normal. He may bring out a toaster and *demonstrate* how he makes toast. You'll know he's desperate to win if he shows how he cut the crust off.

The "real" Al Gore has become an almost mythical figure, a

chimera, a creature with the head and torso of a politician and the lower body of a normal human being. The *Post* published an excellent story this morning on the duality of the vice president, the Public Gore versus the Private Gore, and concluded that they co-exist, with remarkably poor integration. I think this duality actually gives Gore much of his sense of humor. Humor, as repeatedly noted in this space, is a phenomenon that involves overlapping but incompatible frames of reference. The tension caused by the collision of these referential frames is released through laughter. Al Gore's entire life—very stiff politician co-existing with wise-cracking normal guy—is structurally humorous. By strict definition, his life is a joke.

The big danger tonight is that he'll try too hard to deliver the greatest speech by the greatest man and greatest husband and greatest father in the history of the Milky Way Galaxy. Don't be shocked if he tries to get someone to rise from a wheelchair.

Aug. 18

Looks like we got us a contest here. Al Gore and George W. Bush have both given first-rate speeches. Though some of us get mileage out of caricaturing the candidates (Gore's dull, Dubya's dumb), the truth is that neither of these guys is some lame party hack or empty suit. There's no Millard Fillmore in this race. (I don't actually know much about President Millard Fillmore, but over the years, for reasons unknown but probably associated with his name, he's become my go-to-guy when I need an example on deadline of an ineffectual, dweeby president.)

Perhaps this upbeat outlook will fade before my plane gets east of the 100th meridian. We've seen elections get ugly round about Labor Day. We've seen stupid, trivial issues grip a campaign and suck up all the attention. We've seen candidates turn themselves completely over to their strategists and handlers—and after that all we hear are slogans and sound bites. But this election might actually be full of substance, if the American people can stand it.

Bush and Gore are vigorous, confident, and ready to wrassle. Neither man is a Milquetoast. Gore's march to the podium was punctuated by a spectacularly passionate embrace of his wife. Zowie! For a second there I thought we might be getting into V-chip territory. (Note: From my vantage point within the hall, The Kiss, as it would become known, was dramatic, with elements of zoo-animal public mating, but the TV viewers had a close-up view and could better appreciate the face-mashing intensity of the thing.)

Both candidates came up big when they had to. Bush's speech back in Philadelphia was more eloquent—in the sense of being speechwriterly—but Gore's achieved the greater miracle, turning a notoriously mannered politician into an authentic character. A simple line—"I stand before you as my own man"—proved dramatic, a cymbals-crashing declaration of independence from Clinton. The speech was full of policy wonk material, but that's the genuine Gore.

Gore professed humility—acknowledging that his Vietnam War service wasn't that dangerous, for example, and later saying that he would never be the most exciting politician—but he didn't take it too far. He's trying to become president. He has to fill the arena with his passions and ambitions. He knew why he was there, knew the foundation he was operating from, his debt to his parents, his blessings.

To be a presidential nominee is to be anointed a gladiator. Bush and Gore have steeled themselves for the role. They both pump iron maniacally—we've probably never had two candidates in such fighting trim. Bush stood ramrod straight when he delivered his speech in Philadelphia. Gore put a little more body English into his big lines (the passionate words are literally underlined on the TelePrompTer). He'd kind of lurch upward on his tiptoes, as though trying to head a soccer ball. This is physical, heart-pounding, adrenalized work—unless you're Joe Lieberman.

When Lieberman took the stage earlier, he radiated an almost unnatural serenity. He's got so much inner peace he might well have decided to take a nap on stage. He did survey the arena a lot, looking up at the nosebleed sections, as though calmly noting the scale of the hall. He was thinking: "Jeepers. Big room. Neat!"

One of the hardest parts of writing about these people is remembering that they're human beings and not just "material." Of course they are not human beings like everyone else. Some politicians have egos that can fill a place like the Staples Center to the rafters. They walk in, see thousands of people waving pennants with their name on it, hear the cheers, acknowledge the screams of adoration, and think: "Why can't there be more red balloons?"

One night at about 11:00 P.M., outside a party, a top adviser to President Clinton said his cell phone had died. He borrowed mine, called the White House (I confirmed this later by scrolling through the phone's call log), and gave the operator my cell phone number. A few minutes later the call arrived. It was, I realized, from the nation's Talker-in-Chief.

Clinton had flown back to Washington already. His wife was campaigning for the Senate, and he had the house to himself. What do you do when you're the president of the United States, alone at home, at 2:00 A.M. Washington time, in the middle of a Democratic National Convention? You could sleep, conceivably. Or you could stay up really late, calling your advisers on their cell phones at parties in Los Angeles and gabbing about the speeches and the latest poll numbers and whether Gore has the right strategy and so on.

I did not eavesdrop, but I kept an eye on my cell phone. They talked for five minutes . . . ten minutes . . . twelve minutes, thirteen, fourteen . . . Lord have mercy, my batteries were going to die! Shut up already!

Eventually the call was over, and I got my cell phone back. I spent the rest of the night in an agitated state, unable to socialize normally. The big guy at the White House still had my number. He'd probably call again. I might have to interrupt a conversation already in progress—"Excuse me," I'd say calmly, "I need to take this call from the president."

PART THREE

CAMPAIGN

CANDIDATES
IN THE MIST

Gore got his bounce. In the three weeks after the Democratic convention, George W. Bush lost his once-commanding lead. Pundits smelled blood. His campaign was disintegrating, they said. The punditry seemed to be getting ahead of the facts—the polls showed the race still tied. Naturally I had no choice but to weigh in with a declaration that Bush was completely finished and that the only thing left in Campaign 2000 was the technicality of the vote itself. No sooner did the column go up on the site than the raging e-mails came pouring in. Apparently the Bush supporters found my message unamusing. The column was posted at far right Web sites. My words spread through the Net, a thought contagion, a viral explosion of liberal Washington elitism. I was a bad man, I was vile—but I had readers.

Sept. 8

Many times we have warned readers against the mistake of leaping to conclusions, particularly when it comes to presidential campaigns. Polls can't be trusted. Trends evaporate overnight. Yesterday's bumbler is tomorrow's political genius. This is still early September, and Al Gore and George W. Bush have lots of campaigning still ahead of them.

That said, we can now say with conviction that the campaign is over, for all practical purposes. Bush has lost. The ship has hit the iceberg.

On January 20, Albert Arnold Gore XVI will take the oath of office as the forty-third president of the United States.

This is a known fact inside the Beltway. The only people yet to be clued in are the voters themselves, out there in places like Ohio and Missouri. That's a technicality. They'll learn the truth in November.

Bush, too, may be unaware of the demise of his campaign. He has heard carping from fellow Republicans, and he has taken a pounding in the liberal media. His response is to pretend that he's always had the harder task, going against an incumbent. "I am the underdog—I sure am," he said yesterday. "But I was underdog when I first started. Nothing's changed about underdog status."

The problem is, underdogs usually lose. Bush will surely uphold that trend.

Why has Bush failed so badly? Out of habit. Bush has a long history of failure, stumbles, and underachievements—an unfortunate characteristic for someone trying to be elected president.

Let's look closely at the latest *Washington Post*–ABC News poll, published this morning. The first thing you notice is that Pat Buchanan, after more than eight years of campaigning for president, has finally arrived at his proper status, that of asterisk. That means his support is less than half of 1 percent of the likely vote. The peasants with pitchforks must be harvesting the corn crop. Considering his effort, all the noise he has made over the years, he's a major league asterisk.

The next thing you see is that Gore and Bush are dead even. They're both at 47 percent among likely voters.

Admittedly that gives pause to those of us who declare that Bush has ceased to be a credible candidate. It raises the slim possibility that it is premature to declare Bush a bloated, maggot-eaten carcass on the roadside of American politics.

Still, within the *Post*/ABC poll, there are worrisome trends for Bush. Gore's "internals" are much stronger than they used to be, and should gradually translate into an electoral edge. For example, asked who could be trusted on the issue of "improving education and the schools," respondents gave the edge to Gore by a 50 per-

cent to 38 percent margin. On the question of "protecting the Social Security system," Gore again beats Bush by 48 percent to 40
percent. On the matter of "improving the health care system," respondents trusted Gore over Bush by 49 percent to 38 percent.

Bush has had a terrible week, making a big fuss about the kind
of debates he wants, a losing gambit from the start. It's as though
his advisers told him, "Governor, you need to do everything in
your power to make people think you fear Al Gore."

On the stump in recent days he has invented a stunt in which he
waves four dollar bills in the air. He then gives one to someone in
the crowd. This demonstrates that he's using one dollar out of four
of the budget surplus for tax cuts. One "Rough Draft" reader—a
lawyer—points out the clumsiness of this maneuver. First, it looks
like the worst sort of pandering. Vote for me and I'll give you a dollar! Worse yet, one dollar looks so chintzy. If you're going to give
people money, give them a *twenty*.

It is getting late for Bush to put on a surge against a sitting vice
president during an economic boom with the country at peace.
The Olympics start in a week, and that will suck up a lot of attention. At this point, Bush has only one realistic hope. He has to win
the debates—with as large an audience as possible.

Which is why there will be at least three of them, televised on
every network. Just what Al Gore has wanted all along.

*I drove three hundred miles on I-75, which slices down through
the battleground states of Michigan and Ohio. I wanted to talk to
voters. When you go on the road you discover that the American
political mind is all over the place, that it resists any imposition of
order. Also, you discover there's a lot of corn out there.*

Cincinnati
Sept. 13

Chuck Hall, button peddler, is pretty much disgusted. He travels from rally to rally, selling political buttons, like the anti-Bush one saying "Read My Lips—No New Texans," or the one that, possibly designed in an alternate universe, shows Al Gore's smiling face next to Mount Rushmore.

Business is poor. Partly it's the competition—these days there are lots of button-peddling start-ups, rivals who stand a few feet away and sell the same merchandise. But Hall also gets the sense that people don't much care about this campaign, or these candidates. It's not like 1992, when Bill Clinton was the fresh face in politics. "They wanted his button. They wanted *him.*"

Hall stood in a community college parking lot where Al Gore had just finished a stump speech. Gore drew a pretty decent crowd, maybe 1,500 people. Hall sold about twenty-five buttons. He counted out his cash—$97. Not good.

The race for president is nip and tuck, as is the contest for the control of Congress, and yet even here, in this swingingest of swing states, passion is scarce. Gore—who came here to talk about education—is not the kind of candidate who turns apathetic people into feverish political animals. His own eruptions of passion can be jangling. He has the habit of changing registers abruptly—he'll be talking about an education proposal one moment in fairly even tones, then he'll suddenly bellow "ARE YOU WITH ME?" He got more Southern as his speech wore on, as though he remembered how close he was to Kentucky. "You ain't seen nothin' yet!" he shouted.

He's still doing that "populist" thing.

"I'm tellin' you, it's time to take 'em on, take on the big drug companies," he said. "I believe it makes a big difference whose side you're on. I'm on *your* side. I'm on the side of the people."

Gore finished with a move borrowed from a revival tent, asking his listeners to open their hearts and genuinely believe that they can make America a better place. We're all imperfect, he said. We all fall short. But this is still the greatest country on the face of the earth. A surprising eruption of fireworks at the end would have been more spectacular had it not been in the middle of the afternoon.

The best line of the afternoon belonged to Joe Lieberman, who showed up to play the Ed McMahon role. "I'm trying to get my wife to give me a seven-second public kiss," he said.

They didn't even make the lead story on the eleven o'clock news. Over in Indiana, the legendary college basketball coach Bobby Knight had been fired. That was big news in southern Ohio.

My drive south began in Democrat territory, the union stronghold of Flint, Michigan, but down here near the Ohio River it's wall-to-wall Republicans. In the last sixty years the only Democratic presidential candidate to carry the area around Hamilton County was Lyndon Johnson.

Earlier in the day, the vice president visited Middletown, so named because it's halfway between Dayton and Cincinnati. It's so thoroughly Middle America that companies come here to test their consumer products. Gore went to the high school—it's hard to round up a crowd of Democrats in this part of Ohio, but you can always force teenagers to march down to the gym to hear you speak. (A speech at a prison would have also worked, but might have created security problems.)

"I want all of you to be able to reach your full potential by having access to the best education possible," Gore told the students. They struggled to pay attention. The gym was sweltering. The kids in the back of the crowd, near the news media, were nudging each other and giggling and flirting. The vice president spoke about Social Security and prescription drug benefits. He might as well have been speaking in Farsi.

Fortunately for Gore, he had cheerleaders. The squad was in full uniform, propped up in the bleachers right behind him. When he called for a one-dollar raise in the minimum wage, the cheer-leaders shrieked and bounced and waved their purple-and-white pom-poms.

There had to be some votes out there somewhere.

Warsaw, Kentucky
Sept. 15

The bar doubled as a bait shop, and it clung to a hill above a muddy creek that flowed into the Ohio River. Three vehicles were parked outside: a motocycle, a pickup, and a hearse. The hearse had a skull and bones hanging from the rearview mirror. In one window I could see a fake human hand.

It was dark inside the bar. Four men, hard-looking, sat on stools, nursing beers. No proprietor was in sight. The announce-ment of the intrusion of a *Washington Post* reporter was greeted with the same warmth as would be offered an agent from the IRS. Eye contact was minimal. I considered saying, "Gentlemen, why the frosty reception?" but instinct held my tongue.

Responding to a query, the men informed me that they were not politically active.

"I never voted in an election. Probably never will," said the man who drives the hearse. I asked him why he drove such a vehi-cle. For laughs, he said.

This was one of those interviews that did not yield bountiful data. As I left the bar, someone called out, "You be careful out there!" He employed the tone you'd use on someone with a "Kill Me" sign stuck on his back.

That was about the point I decided I was tired of man-on-the-street journalism. By now I'd talked to sports fans at the Super-dome in Detroit (a football game) and at Cinergy Field in Cincinnati (baseball), college liberals in a café in Ann Arbor, the big union guys in Flint, the high school kids in Middletown, and various people at truck stops and waffle houses and watering holes along I-75. What I learned during my long drive is something I should have already known: There's all types out there. To put together a winning majority, or even a plurality, in a national election means selling yourself to an incredible variety of folks, from the highly religious to the severely intellectual to the barely conscious, from people who care about a single specific issue (guns, abortion, school vouchers) to people who will make their decision based on a dream they have the night before they go to the polls. We tend to mock the polls, but at least the polls impose a coherence on the scattered thinking of the American people.

When you ask people how they'll vote, usually they'll blurt out the answer as though it's obvious—as though only a complete imbecile would consider any other possibility. Political views emerge from life experience. If you're Frank Benson, a union officer up in Flint, you've seen massive layoffs at the Ford plant. You've seen the equipment you've worked on for years suddenly shipped to Mexico. You're never going to like a candidate who's a friend of Big Business. Benson said of Bush, "He's a lot of smoke. He's an oil man. He's a millionaire oil man. And his running partner is a millionaire oil man."

But even a simplistic rule—union members like Gore—doesn't hold up to scrutiny. Leon Masengale, a retired Kellogg's millwright, is a Republican and loyal Rush Limbaugh listener who thinks Gore is acting like Santa Claus: "The Democrats are promising them everything under the sun. Free medicine, free insurance, free drugs. Democrats promise to take care of you from the cradle to the grave. Never have to worry about anything."

Some conservatives, I noticed, sound persecuted. They speak as though they are members of a secret society of logical citizens, surrounded by oceans of socialists, media liberals, shakedown artists, criminals, psychiatric patients, men-hating feminists, and various other freaks of nature. They're trapped in a culture gone insane.

Here's Stephen Smith, a telephone company manager: "I believe in the family values. With the entertainment industry, the liberal society has ruined the young people of America. Programs like *Roseanne,* you got young people talking back to their parents, they sass their parents. You got the homosexual shows that took over the Emmys. To me that's a disgrace."

People kept talking to me about guns. Gore would take them away. That's what they'd heard. "I don't like nobody tellin' me I cain't have no guns. Takes away your freedom to bear arms," said Charlie Williford, a welder who normally votes Democratic but plans to vote for Bush.

Pat McGuire, a freight handler at the Cincinnati airport, just wants to keep her streak alive. Since she reached voting age she's voted for Ronald Reagan twice, George Bush once, and Bill Clinton twice—winners every time. She's planning this time to vote for Bush. She says, "I could live with Gore, but I think Bush is going to win."

She doesn't really have a beef with the Democrats. "We've had some good times with Clinton the past eight years. I mean, he's a weirdo, but life is good. I think we should actually vote for that dude on *The West Wing.* Martin Sheen. I love that guy!"

Mylinda Dummit, here in northern Kentucky, is one of the undecideds. "It's gonna be a hunch," she told me as she wielded a leaf-blower on her front sidewalk. Dummit—she pronounces her first name "My Linda"—is on the town council in Glencoe. Dummit's house is the one with the sign saying "Dale Earnhardt Fan Club Parking Only" (and across the street from the house with the Ten Commandments posted on the front lawn).

Dummit has voted for Republicans and Democrats in the past. She's not sure yet about Bush and Gore. She kind of likes Bush.

"I'm not saying I wouldn't change my mind on the last day," she said. "As a woman, there's hunches. There's just things you feel about people."

The race is very close. Bush and Gore have to pound the pavement, motivate their friends, steal a vote here and there. And hope the hunches go their way.

Oil prices had skyrocketed. Gore proposed a solution: Tap into the Strategic Oil Reserve, which had been created for use in wars and national emergencies. Clinton did just that the next day. The move succeeded in triggering a decrease in oil prices, but Gore's critics said he was guilty of pandering. Many of us had simultaneously noticed that Gore's recent two-hundred-page economic plan had promised to end virtually all forms of human suffering. If you had a problem, he had a government program to solve it.

Sept. 25

Vice President Al Gore, appearing this morning on NBC's *Today* show, announced that his first priority as president would be to distribute gold bricks from Fort Knox to every middle-class family in America. He also vowed to combat rising aluminum foil prices by releasing part of the federal government's Strategic Foil Reserve.

"We live in a nation in which a typical family can no longer afford to wrap a baked potato in foil," Gore said. "That must change. I will take on Big Foil. Under my administration, foil will be cheaper than paper towels. You will wrap your potato in foil and, when fully baked, slather it with real butter and giant dollops of sour cream. You will have bacon bits! You will have whatever you want, more than you ever dreamed. When I'm president, the motto of this great country will be Try Some Cheese on That."

Challenged by interviewer Matt Lauer, Gore denied he was pandering. He said he was far too busy watching NBC's brilliant coverage of the Olympics. He promised Lauer that, under a Gore administration, NBC's coverage of the 2004 Olympics in Athens would have "fantastic" ratings, even if it means asking the Justice Department to shut down all other television networks.

"I can get you a 26 rating with a 43 share, Matt. I can get you *Survivor* numbers," the vice president said.

Republican candidate George W. Bush, campaigning in Guam, said Gore's latest series of promises were "truly abdominal."

"You let bureaucrats give you foil, next thing, they've got the wax paper," Bush said. "They've got the freezer bags. Knives and forks. Then they get our guns. Heck yeah I'm ticked off. I'm interrogated."

Bush campaign officials in Austin, asked to translate the governor's words, released a statement saying Bush was fatigued from playing thirty-six holes on Sunday.

Gore is seeking to get his campaign back on track after a series of recent stumbles. At a fund-raiser last week, Gore and his running mate, Joe Lieberman, praised Hollywood movie moguls for their creative genius and performed a well-received skit in which Lieberman, dressed in a hockey mask and wielding a chain saw, chased Gore out of the building. Gore later vowed that, as president, all movies will have a G rating "regardless of content."

Gore also struggled with the so-called "dog" issue. It happened after he told a story about his mother-in-law paying three times more for an arthritis medication than what his family pays to give the same drug to his dog, Shiloh. Investigative journalists tracked down the details of the situation and learned that the dog was a "composite." Gore spent several days hedging when asked if he really had a dog.

"I definitely have a mother-in-law. And I know many people who have dogs," Gore said in his defense. "If we accept the premise that I have a dog, we can rest assured that it would certainly be a severely arthritic dog. This dog, real or imagined, can barely crawl across the room. And although I personally am too busy to attend to the needs of an animal companion, I have an able staff that informs me of any medical needs of the creatures in my environment. Therefore the anecdote comports with the truth as we can ascertain it presently."

Although a few right-wing pundits and radio talk show hosts assailed Gore for his "legalistic" language, the news media in general agreed to let the dog story die after Gore campaign officials pointed out that any additional negative coverage could hurt Gore in the polls.

Campaign aides in Nashville, spinning the situation, pointed out that Gore is not a "natural politician," and has difficulty with the basic requirement of believing his own lies. Gore, they said, still chuckles nervously just before he utters a stretcher.

"He has studied at the feet of the master for eight years, and still doesn't quite get it," one aide said. "He's improving. We think for a moment he actually believed the dog anecdote was true."

Sept. 27

"Al Gore's presidential campaign suspended a junior staffer yesterday after he acknowledged boasting of a 'mole' planted in Texas Governor George W. Bush's campaign." — The Washington Post, *Sept. 24*

The governor entered his private office with the wariness of a burglar. He opened a desk drawer. Five . . . ten . . . fifteen . . . eighteen paper clips. Same as yesterday. He looked under the desk. He checked behind the curtains. He scanned the ceiling. Wasn't there a crawl space above the acoustic ceiling tiles? And what about the air ducts? Perhaps the mole had a . . . what would you call it . . . cloak of invisibility. One of those *physics* things. Or is that just make-believe? "Shoulda studied," George W. Bush said out loud.

He sniffed the air. Perhaps the mole wore a certain cologne or perfume. The mole might carry traceable smells on his or her shoes. The governor got on his knees and sniffed the floor like a dog.

"Governor?" said a voice. It was Phigglesworth, the campaign logistician. "It's time for debate practice."

Bush hated debate practice. Everyone so *nitpicky*. Gotta be commanding. Masterful. But can't insult. The ladies don't like it.

Can't smirk. How the heck do you not smirk when smirking is what the muscles around your face do naturally? Especially around Democrats! Bunch of liberal *weenies*. The governor suddenly caught himself smirking, and clamped his hands over his face to rearrange his expression.

The only part of debate practice he liked was the handshake training, where they taught you how to crush your opponent's fingers like they're Chinese fortune cookies. He'd show that Mr. Smartypants who was top dog!

The governor arrived at the practice room and recoiled at what he saw. The room was full of staffers, flunkies, technicians, makeup gals, fussy folks, full-time hand-wringers with pursed lips. He barely knew half of 'em. Even the campaign pros, they were just hired guns—you looked in their eyes and didn't really know for sure you had a Republican staring back. Things go south, they run to their liberal media buddies. Call you dumb behind your back. Only people he could trust were the members of his immediate family. He wished Jeb were around. Hard to even get Jeb on the phone lately, for some reason.

He took his position behind the podium. A few feet away, "Al Gore" was played by a senator with twigs and leaves stuck into his hair.

The governor began his opening monologue. He had some new ideas he wanted to play around with.

"My fellow 'mericans. I have something very disturbin' to talk about. My opponent. Very disturbin' man. His campaign has put a MOLE in my operation. This is an indespicable act. The FBI is asking questions and I will cooperate fully. We need to ask the question, 'What did I know, and when will I know it?' I'm not dodging anything. Don't even look at me. Ask him, over there, the Gore fella. Always blaming others, using SCARE TACTICS, trying to create FEAR in the ELDERLY. I want to . . ."

Later, at the staff meeting, reviews were lukewarm. It was generally agreed that the governor should not "freelance," as the campaign pros put it.

The campaign manager then ran through the latest poll numbers, headlines from major papers, the schedule. The governor tried to concentrate, but could only think of the mole. The betrayer! In his mind he called him The Red. A communist, possibly. Red September, that's the code name. Like the Clancy book. Good writer, Clancy. All that nifty hardware. Ships and planes. Aircraft carriers. Submarines.

" . . . concerns about the Florida operation," the campaign manager was saying. The governor snapped to attention. Why was everyone always so concerned about Florida?

A news clipping was passed around. There was a picture of the governor with his brother. *Some Republicans question Jeb's lack of campaigning,* the caption said.

He had a thought, a flash in the brain. He instantly banished it.

It came back an hour later, when, glancing through some briefing papers, he saw an analysis of the electoral college. Florida had mysteriously gone from a Bush lock to a toss-up. *Florida.* And why hadn't Jeb returned his call?

Two hours later he was lurching, alone, through a dark garage. He kept both arms in front of him, outstretched like a zombie. He did not want to walk into a pillar. He could barely see the shapes of parked cars. He cursed the darkness. He felt like a mole himself. He had become the Mole Man, confined to the underworld. Were it not for the intense fear of being recognized he would have taken off his sunglasses.

"Good evening, Governor," said a voice from nowhere. Spinning, heart pounding, Bush saw a match flare. It stroked the tip of a cigarette that led to the mouth of a figure with the collar of his trench coat pulled up around his ears.

"Hello, Control," the governor said.

Bush always hated the way Control snuck up on him, the way

he insisted on meeting in dark garages, his penchant for code names, secret handshakes, all that old Skull and Bones stuff.

"Who is he? How deep does it go?" the governor asked, practically gasping.

"I think you know," said Control.

"What are you saying?" said the governor. "Tell me. Come on, Dad, I'm tired of the games!"

Control paused. He hated to see his son so pathetic.

"Of course it's Jeb. Don't be foolish, son. It's been this way since you were little boys. You got the glory. He was second fiddle. He had the brains and the looks, you had the charm and the swagger. You always wound up with the pick of the chick, he got a drumstick. I guess it's payback time for Jebbie."

"Dad, with your permission I'm going to give him so many noogies on his fat skull he's going to—"

"No need to do anything, son. I took care of it. For the duration of the campaign, Jeb's grounded."

The presidential candidates would debate three times over the course of two weeks. Gore showed up at the first debate in heavy makeup that made him look slightly monstrous. He was one eager beaver—over the course of ninety minutes, Gore lectured, hectored, and interrupted. He sighed repeatedly. When it was over, people forgot what the candidates said—but they remembered the sighs. Bush hadn't really won the debate, but Gore, without doubt, had lost it.

Oct. 4

For almost ninety minutes, the debate between presidential candidates Al Gore and George W. Bush remained civil and substantive. Then Bush challenged the character and credibility of Gore. Gore responded by pointing out that Bush had challenged his character and credibility, and said that, although he was emotionally injured, he would not, in turn, challenge Bush's own "highly questionable character" and "overall fraudulence."

The debate then quickly degenerated. Bush said Gore was "a mind-numbing bore." Gore called Bush a "dumbass." Bush cringed at this remark and accused Gore of being "an aging pot-head." Gore, obviously prepared for the barb, produced a whiskey bottle from behind the rostrum and said, tauntingly, "Thirsty, George?" The ensuing melee and police intervention shocked veteran political analysts and brought the evening to a disturbing conclusion.

Focus groups interviewed by the major networks generally agreed that Bush closed the so-called "stature gap" by breaking free of Gore's headlock and momentarily forcing the vice president's face to the floor. Some viewers believed, however, that Bush's clumsy jabs at Gore's eyeballs, as well as Gore's attempt to bite Bush on the nose, amounted to "unpresidential" behavior.

I have watched every major televised debate since Lincoln-Douglas and will say with conviction that this bizarre ending relieved what was an otherwise insipid evening. We now understand why NBC gave its affiliates the choice between broadcasting the debate or carrying extremely delayed videotape of the women's 10-meter synchronized diving. Fox executives ignored the debate entirely, instead airing a new installment of the network's hit show, *America's Funniest Autopsies*.

The debate ground rules did not allow for direct exchanges between the candidates. Under the rules, however, the candidates were allowed to leer at each other, snort, scoff, growl, shake their heads in dismay, gasp, flap their hands frantically as though they smelled something bad, and stick their fingers down their throats in a mocking gesture to suggest intense nausea.

The Bush campaign at the end of the night released a statement accusing Gore of "subliminal sighing" whenever Bush spoke. The Gore campaign responded by saying that this was "yet another personal attack" and that Gore was merely doing Pranayama breathing exercises taught to him by his personal guru, Swami Swickijananda of Sausalito, California.

"The vice president was not sighing, but was merely exhaling forcefully to realign the *chi* energy within his body," the statement said.

Both candidates prepared for the debate in their characteristic fashions. Bush studied the dictionary and the encyclopedia, and memorized the names of American presidents and the capitals of foreign countries. Gore suntanned in Florida until his face attained an unnatural, rubbery, masklike texture.

Both sides knew Gore's battle plan: irritate Bush into submission. Bush for the most part kept his cool. Many analysts said Bush was the winner simply by not mangling the English language or claiming that Poland is in Africa. Gore tried to incite a pronunciation catastrophe by the Texas governor when he mentioned the opposition leader in Serbia—Kostunica—but Bush saw the verbal land mine and gingerly stepped around it.

At one point the vice president took credit for winning the war in Kosovo. He said he "took a risk" when he invited the former prime minister of Russia and the head of Finland to his mansion and asked them to negotiate the surrender of Serbia. Gore pointed out that he soldiered through the risky evening even when the navy stewards ran out of vodka and the Russians and Finns became unruly.

Gore pounded Bush with numbers. At one point the vice president declared, "Of the 30 percent of my opponent's tax cut that goes to the richest 1 percent of Americans, 70 percent is for the 0.5 percent who are more than three standard deviations from the mean per capita income." Bush responded with a congenial laugh, saying, "Numbers, shnumbers."

Unclear was whether Gore scored any points by mentioning ordinary people, some of whom were in the audience last night and have become unofficial advisers to the campaign. Winnifred

Skinner is the Iowa retiree who picks up cans on the side of the road and uses the deposit money to pay for her medication. Gore announced that, in his administration, Skinner will be secretary of the treasury.

Polls taken before, during, and after the debate show no major shift toward either candidate. Undecided voters interviewed on television after the debate offered a variety of opinions that, experts agreed, were irrational and disconnected from reality. Researchers are now interviewing these undecided voters to determine what is preventing them, even at this late date, from making up their minds.

Gore's brain is like the sound system on an airplane. He's got some classical music up there, some rock and roll, some country, and a steady commentary from air traffic controllers. The challenge for Gore has always been to figure out which channel he should let his audiences hear.

I saw him in 1992 in Rio, at the Earth Summit, before he was picked as Bill Clinton's running mate. He was speaking in a circus-sized tent set up for all the alternative summiteers, the enviros and feminists and Buddhists and various indigenous peoples. Gore was channeling his inner preacher ... shouting, imploring, waving his arms, testifying to the environmental emergency facing the planet earth. He was on fire. His shirt was soaked. He was a true believer.

We've all seen another Gore, the Beta Male. Cautious. Diplomatic. E-nun-ci-a-ting his words. This is the Gore so well bred he is physically unable to fidget. This is the Gore who showed up for the second debate. He did not sigh or roll his eyes. He was well behaved and deferential—to a fault.

I happened to be in Colorado, in the mountains. I'd been out among the rutting elk, and couldn't decide if I should file a column about the presidential debate or about these noisy mammals going through their mating rituals. Or could the subjects be combined?

Estes Park, Colorado
Oct. 12

The horse tranquilizers injected into the vice president will have worn off by now. He is likely to be in a bad mood. He desperately wants to be president, but after two debates he's perfectly positioned himself to return to the private sector.

They might take him back at the Nashville paper. If so, I doubt he'd get his old investigative reporter slot. That job requires too much attention to detail. He might consider becoming a lobbyist, a rainmaker, but after watching him in these debates it's not clear that persuasiveness is his strong suit. He'd definitely make a good schoolteacher. In a happy coincidence, George W. Bush says he wants to improve our schools and have better teachers. It'd be an excellent time for Gore to apply!

It's possible that the veep did better last night than I thought he did. My impression may be skewed by my current location, in the Rocky Mountains, amid the rutting elk.

This is the bugling season. The males start strutting around shortly before dusk, showing off their antlers, being studly. Every minute or so a bull will emit a prolonged, keening noise, rising in pitch, a Gershwinesque note that is sometimes bracketed with a bit of woofing and snorting.

These animals are presidential. They know what they think. They reek of confidence, brio, and elk urine (the males wet themselves, I'm told, as part of the mating ritual). They are unflappable, and care not that human beings are pulling up in cars to observe. They have no handlers, no makeup artists, no pollsters. I think I've made my point. It's probably a stupid point, but there it is. I fear that the vice president did not compare favorably to the elk. His bugling is weak.

Gore seemed intent on being inoffensive last night, and inoffensive is not the same thing as being presidential. He was running last night against both his opponent, the Texas governor, and the overbearing Al Gore of last week. Gore was almost too nice. He seemed a bit wishy-washy. Discussing foreign policy, he lapsed into the dreaded Mr. Rogers speech pattern. He exuded caution. You could see him reining in his urges; when he looked at Bush he was a cat on a windowsill eyeing a bird.

On the issue of gun control, Gore delivered his message as though his number one priority was to avoid upsetting hunters and sportsmen in the Midwest. He mentioned the student shootings at Columbine High School in Littleton, Colorado, and the plague of cheap handguns, but he never really got passionate about what is surely a national tragedy, an epidemic of gun violence. Carefully crafted, nuanced answers have their place, and a presidential debate is not one of them.

Gore even admitted making mistakes last week, saying, "I'm sorry about that and I'm going to try to do better." This is bugling at its feeblest. Presidents typically don't go around saying they'll try to do better. Even when they make a colossal mistake they stick to their guns. We all saw what it took to get Bill Clinton to admit to a personal error. Maybe Gore will get points with sensitive swing voters who want a president who will admit to fallibility. Maybe that line was a major hit. In coming days it could become Gore's mantra. "I will try to do better!" he will shout on the stump. "I will strive to improve my lame performance!"

Bush, meanwhile, had a good night. He didn't have the deer-in-the-headlights problem of last week. He seemed to know what he believed and he said it with gusto. When it comes to foreign policy expertise he's not exactly George Kennan, but he didn't hurt himself. Last week you got the impression that, in a crisis, the first thing he'll do is dial Kennebunkport and scream "Daaad!" Bush this time sounded like a pragmatic thinker. Gore would solve the world's problems by telling people how they could be more like us. Bush would be more "humble," wouldn't do any of that "nation building" stuff. Bush understands that Americans don't really like the rest of the world, and would prefer that it went away, except for the better vacation spots.

Bush said, a couple of times, "I'm not sure where the vice president is coming from." Meaning, the vice president is coming from left field, from Mars, from the asteroid belt. Bush also preempted criticism that he can't speak the English language. "I've been known to mangle a syl-LAB-le or two. If you know what I mean," he said. This was bad news for humorists. If he starts making fun of himself, it's tantamount to stealing our material.

It's impossible to know what will remain in voters' minds from these debates. Will they think Bush sounded tough-minded and practical when he talked about putting the killers of James Byrd to death? Or will they think he sounded brutal, like a good ol' boy who's callous about human life? (Or will they focus on something superficial, like the configuration of his lips, the gradual mutation of his smirk?)

Contaminating everything is the suspicion that both candidates are being less than completely forthcoming. Everything's so targeted. They know exactly which swing voters in which districts in which states they want to lure over to their column. Just once during one of these debates I wish a candidate would turn to the moderator and say, "Incidentally, Jim, we're just saying whatever we have to say to eke out a narrow electoral college majority. None of this is what we *really* think."

The final debate was in a town hall format. Gore returned to his former, aggressive style. He looked like he wanted to pull a Hannibal Lecter on Bush: eat him with fava beans and a nice Chianti.

Oct. 18

This will go down in history as the "Mine Is Bigger Than Yours" debate. It was a weirdly physical event, a ninety-minute strut-off. Gore in particular was constantly zooming around the room, pivoting, twirling, flashing tail feathers. He was apparently coached by a body linguist, or perhaps by an anthropologist who specializes in primate display rituals. Never before in a presidential campaign have we seen so much monkey behavior. This was "Candidates in the Mist."

Bush snickered and smirked but occasionally seemed ready to flee. He was trapped in a cage with a chest-beating gorilla. His only possible survival tactic was the Rope-a-Dope, letting Gore punch himself into exhaustion. Gore combined his physical intimidation with SuperNerd zingers, such as, "What about the Dingell-Norwood bill?"

Gore smiled as he asked the question. He knows so much more about the Dingell-Norwood bill than Bush. Gore is going to adopt this question as his battle cry. WHAT ABOUT DINGELL-NORWOOD? Catchy, and totally eviscerating.

No doubt millions of people held their breath in that nerve-wracking moment when Alpha Gore invaded Bush's physical space. This wasn't some spontaneous, inadvertent maneuver. Gore clearly had decided, before the debate, that he would be a Space Invader. Bush whirled and nodded curtly, slightly alarmed. For a second you didn't know what would happen. Would Gore actually hit Bush? Is it possible we've come to that?

We've seen some embarrassing moments in American politics of late—a general loss of dignity, a White House sex scandal, an unsavory impeachment drama, the constant groveling by our leaders for campaign contributions—and there's a general sense that things have changed, that the system has been debased. I think we would not be that shocked if one candidate popped another with a quick jab to the face.

This debate was unlike anything we've seen before. Most debates since 1960 have been essentially talking head events, the candidates securely affixed to a podium. The "town hall" format arrived only in 1992, but there were three candidates on stage (Bill Clinton, Bush the Elder, and Ross Perot), and it didn't have that gladiator feel. This time we kept expecting Bush and Gore to take turns saying, "I am Spartacus."

Once again we wait to see how the debate will play in the public at large. I thought Gore dominated Bush quite effectively, though some viewers might have been repulsed by the Godzilla routine.

Last night's debate was good television, and maybe it was a good forum for assessing leadership qualities. But you wonder where this is all going. There was a time when candidates were just names and faces, serving as fronts for political parties. The entire campaign lasted a matter of weeks. Over time, the process has mutated and evolved into a two-year clash of titans, heavy on theater and posturing. It's all so personal. It's even more personal on our end, the voters' side. We have little loyalty to party. We're a nation of wimpy individualists wondering what we're going to get from our government.

The American presidency has become a cult of personality that Stalin would envy. We know more about Bill Clinton than we want to know; his most embarrassing transgressions are documented, with footnotes. It takes a certain kind of garrulous, shameless, exhibitionist personality to fill the job. Clinton this week has already tried to broker Middle East peace in Egypt, attended a memorial service for slain sailors, raised funds for a congressional candidate, and this afternoon will schmooze with Tiger Woods and his fellow golfers. And I believe it's still only Wednesday.

As part of this evolving political system we now require our candidates to stage these town hall events where they show that they can interact with ordinary citizens in a human-to-human manner. What results is a performance, a dance, each candidate trying out certain steps, approaching the questioner, beaming empathy, then turning to the opponent to attack this impostor, this imbecile, this very bad man who would ruin our country. Over time this system puts intense selection pressure on the candidate pool, favoring peacocks and poseurs.

Projected into the future, we see where the system is heading: A Death Match. Two men in a ring. The last one breathing wins.

The race was deadlocked. Bush had a slight lead in most polls, but his lead was often just three or four or five points, within the poll's margin of error. I drove to Pennsylvania to take the pulse of a crucial battleground state. From the highway I saw farms and factories. It's always enchanting to escape Washington and go places where people actually work for a living, rather than simply talk on the phone and send faxes and attend conferences and take expense account lunches featuring salads made of incredibly precious hand-crafted organic free range lettuces. The highlight of the trip was the sign at the Maryland border, put up by Maryland authorities: "We Enjoyed Your Company." It was true, I had been good company. But how did they know?

Oct. 24

Just east of the Susquehanna River I saw a sign for a convent, the Adorers of the Blood of Christ. My policy is to avoid disturbing nuns in their cloister, except when I am desperate for material. Minutes later I was sitting across a desk from Sister Eugene Boyich.

The presidential campaign seemed an odd thing to mention. Pennsylvania is a battleground state, twenty-three electoral votes in the balance, with tracking polls showing George W. Bush and Al Gore almost dead even. But did the Precious Blood Sisters care about such matters? Was the topic not slightly vulgar? Weren't they focused on timeless, spiritual concerns? Apprehensively, I asked Sister Eugene if she had a preference in the presidential race.

"Definitely! From the very beginning. Bush!"

My prejudices were shattered. The nuns are fully engaged in the process and will probably vote in higher percentages than most citizens.

"Bush can bring people together. A coalition. To me, that's very important, because we're always quarreling about something and no one seems to have the unity," said Sister Eugene, who unlike some of the other sisters did not wear a habit. She noted, however, that Bush's pro-life position is "inconsistent," as it applies to the unborn but not to the criminally convicted. The Holy Father is quite explicit in his disapproval of the death penalty.

Several nuns came in to pick up their mail, and Sister Eugene polled them. Two wanted Gore, two wanted Bush. Sister Mary Alma Dujmic noted that she had just been listening to Rush Limbaugh on the radio.

I asked them what they thought about President Clinton.

"Uh-uh. Uh-uh," Sister Eugene said, shaking her head. "His morality alone."

"I feel so sorry for the guy," said Sister Mary Alma.

Sister Eugene said, "He's so intelligent. But he's not sincere. His life is a lie, almost. He's trying to have a legacy, with his foreign policy; but it's too late, he spent too much time fooling around with his girlfriend."

But then Sister Rosemarie Tomak came by, and she defended Clinton. A bit of a debate broke out. Sister Eugene was driving a hard line, but Sister Rosemarie was saying the scandal was over, old news, that Clinton made some mistakes but did right by the country. "He not only made mistakes, he was a liar!" Sister Eugene interjected.

It got a little hot in the room—this was on the verge of turning into *Hardball*. I had sparked dissension in the convent!

The nuns told me not to worry, that they could handle the political debate. I was not an instigator of strife. As I left, Sister Eugene chuckled and said, "I hope I didn't scandalize you."

I drove east, into the heart of Amish country, to a country store in Bird-in-Hand. Behind the counter, Kathy Hondares said she liked Bush and expected him to carry the state, because of "the gun control bugaboo." Lots of hunters in Pennsylvania, she said. "I heard stories, that in England, now that the government has taken their guns away, people are coming into their houses and robbing them."

The Amish don't vote much. One young guy, just in from cutting corn stalks behind a team of four horses, smiled when I asked about the election. He won't vote, he said. "It's just politics," he said.

As the young farmer spoke, a late-model sedan drove by and slowed down. A tourist leaned out the window and snapped his picture. The Amish farmers live their lives as though on a stage. People drive for hundred of miles to see people riding in wagons and not using electricity. There are antiques and crafts stores every few hundred feet, and some kind of Disneyfied tourist attraction called the Amish Experience.

Horse-drawn buggies roll down the sides of the country roads, but some are filled with tourists who have paid money to act like an Amish person for an hour. Someday it will be this exploitation of the authentic that is itself the great marvel and attraction that will draw tourists from far away. People will want to see these strange entrepreneurs who sell overpriced mass-produced crafts in someone else's historic village. They'll want to imagine what it would be like to be operate a tourist attraction. They'll pay thirty bucks a pop to get into a theme park called Commercialization World.

I drove east into Chester County, where high-tech industries have sprung up in the shadow of the steel mills. The population is booming. Valley Forge is nearby—something historic happened there once, some soldiers got cold, these details get fuzzy over time.

In Frazer, pharmaceutical industry folks were holding a business gathering at a hotel. They don't like Gore.

"Al Gore does not seem real."

"To me he has no personality whatsoever. There's no spark in his eyes."

"Gore wants to get licenses and registration for every gun owner. It's the Second Amendment. Who are Clinton and Gore to take these rights away?"

"They say there's a book out there about Gore being like Hitler."

The temptation, as the night grows late, is to argue these points (like Hitler? Did Hitler also have a Jewish running mate?). But sometimes it's best to avoid parsing a statement. There are no tests at the polling booth, no required essays or discussion groups. You don't have to defend your vote, don't have to offer any explanation at all. An intelligent vote counts no more than an irrational one. It's the American way.

Somewhere Along I-78 in Pennsylvania
Oct. 25

A bad smell forced me off the road. It slammed into the car without warning, not a skunk smell but something mysterious, an organic brew with a note of fermentation, rotten apples, rioting bacteria. There are some odors so bad you can't even drive through them; this one was as catastrophic as a flat tire. I pulled off the highway and into a gas station straight out of a Hopper painting.

"There's a pig farm four miles thataway. That's what that is," said the man working the single set of pumps. He was David Fabich, forty-eight, and this was the village of Schubert.

There are three pig farms nearby that "recycle" food waste, he said. A mechanic, Tom Moorehead, pulled up his truck, heard us talking, and said, "It's a landfill, basically." They weren't happy fellows. When the wind blows a certain way, their town stinks.

In such moments you can see the allure of politics, why people drop their private lives and venture across the American countryside pledging to be great leaders and do-gooders and problem-solvers. It would be a great ego trip to be able to pull into a town like Schubert and say, "I can make your town smell better!"

You can also see how people would get cynical about politicians. They hear promises of a better life. They hear reassurances and happy talk. And yet their lives remain a struggle, money is still tight, they can barely breathe. The situation changes, but the emotion is similar all over the place—everywhere I've gone I've heard cynical assessments of politicians, and specifically of Al Gore and George W. Bush.

Fabich, for example, said of Gore and Bush, "They're both politicians, which is just about one stop above used car salesman." He might vote for the Libertarian candidate, Harry Browne.

Moorehead said he would vote for Bush. "Don't trust Gore at all. Too much of the chameleon factor going on. He makes himself into whatever people want to hear."

I drove down the street to the Seven Star Hotel. It's actually a bar, more than a century old. Any hint of the antique and the quaint was sledgehammered by the heavy metal roar of the jukebox. People were shouting at each other from adjacent stools. Loud as it was, someone cranked the volume yet again. I recognized the vocal stylings of the lead singer of AC/DC, who always sounds like someone being tortured with a dentist's drill.

At one corner of the bar, two men, flushed, were having an animated conversation about crooks and liars. They were going full throttle, just raging away, arms flailing. Since they were clearly talking politics I sensed an interview would be appropriate.

The larger of the men told me, "I'm not going to vote for anybody. They're all crooks! They say whatever you want to hear, so they get your vote, and after that, you're *nobody* again."

This was Dwayne Fabich, brother of the man back at the gas station. The other, a thin guy with long hair, wearing a "Reading Motorcycle Club" T-shirt, wouldn't identify himself—nor, considering his dyspeptic demeanor, did I press him to do so. When I told him I was amazed at the cynicism about politicians I had been hearing as I traveled across Pennsylvania, he reared back in shock.

"You're AMAZED? Why are you AMAZED? They're a bunch of communists! The cops can do anything they want, bust anyone for anything!"

A third man, detecting a ruckus, came over to share his own disaffection with the system. He said they were hunters. They'd been hunting that very day. He showed me bloodstains on his hands. Or maybe that was from when the last reporter came into the bar to do interviews.

"We want our guns and we want to keep them. Gore's gotta go," Fabich said.

"They're going to take your guns so they can keep running over you," ventured his long-haired pal.

The conversation proceeded thus, while the lead singer of AC/DC appeared to be enduring a stint on the rack. The Seven Star Hotel was a colorful place, but personally I am more in my element at a Holiday Inn.

Earlier in the day I was in Reading, an old industrial town on the Schuylkill River, its clothing mills long ago converted to factory outlet malls. I stopped in at the outlets and wandered the aisles of discount clothing. People come from hundreds of miles away for the chance to buy $3 brassieres and $4 jeans. The women are in constant motion while their husbands park themselves on benches and at picnic tables. The nonshopper can become disoriented in the blizzard of brand names; it's best to sit still and breathe deeply.

Bill Heffner, a retired baker, said of Gore, "He seems like a sleazy character, crying and whining all the time. I'm not saying Bush is that great a man, but Gore is no man at all."

A lot of people seem to doubt Gore's mettle. Years ago there was cynical talk about the "wimp factor" possibly hurting the chances of another vice president, George H. W. Bush. Somehow

Gore, who volunteered for Vietnam, who is famously aggressive in debates, still reminds some folks of a jelly doughnut.

Downtown Reading has some exquisite architecture, rehabbed during the 1990s, but it still looks like a city left behind, a place where things might get worse before they get better. Shawnya Becton, twenty-two, flanked by her two sons, said of Bush, "It doesn't seem like he's for helping people." She sells insurance by phone, though she herself wouldn't be eligible to buy it, since she doesn't have a Visa or MasterCard.

A man nearby was hawking his own CDs, club music he had recorded here in town, stuff he calls "New Age disco." David Palermo is twenty-six and likes Clinton, will probably vote for Gore. Mostly, though, he wants to sell people his CD at a bargain price of five bucks a pop. He wants to leave this town behind. "I've got two little girls. I'm trying to get out so bad."

Eventually I found a Nader voter, Brenda Hartman. She's an environmentalist who's interested in animal rights. She's worried about Bush winning; if the election is tight she'll switch her vote to Gore instead of Nader.

I found her in a pagoda. It's on the hill above the downtown. It's known simply as the Reading Pagoda, and was built by some oddball nearly a century ago. It's the second-biggest tourist attraction around, after the factory outlets. (I am not trying to suggest that all Ralph Nader supporters work in pagodas, or that all of the people who work in pagodas support Nader. Draw that inference at your own risk.)

From the pagoda's observatory deck you can peer through one of those old-fashioned motorized binoculars that cost a quarter and make a whirring noise. You can scan the valley below and see thousands of row houses, railyards, a kid kicking a ball up the street, a woman taking in her laundry, the struggling downtown, the vast mills turned to shopping meccas, the river, the distant hills turned gold and red at the peak of autumn.

You want to gather it all in, to see and know everything that's going on, to get a grip on where all this is going and what can be done to make it a more beautiful place. But then the shutter closes with a sudden click. Time's up.

"The widow of Democratic Governor Mel Carnahan today vowed to take her husband's dreams to Washington by accepting an appointment to the Senate if Missouri voters pick his name over Republican incumbent John Ashcroft in next week's election. . . . Invoking the memory of the governor in what is shaping up as one of the strangest Senate elections in U.S. political history, Jean Carnahan said the people of Missouri still have a choice to vote for Mel Carnahan. . . .

Over the weekend volunteers had worked to mail more than 750,000 letters to Democrats statewide asking them to continue Mel Carnahan's legacy by voting his name Nov. 7. The campaign has distributed buttons that say 'I'm still with Mel,' and independent groups have circulated pins in the shape of a torch and have added black ribbons to Mel Carnahan yard signs."—The Washington Post, *October 31*

Oct. 31

In a controversial gamble to boost his bid for the White House, Vice President Al Gore today dropped Joe Lieberman as his running mate and replaced him with the most popular Democrat in America, deceased Missouri Governor Mel Carnahan.

"Mel, though biologically defunct, continues to offer the kind of leadership this country needs in the new millennium," Gore said while campaigning in Oregon. "As I myself have shown, the lack of a pulse is no disqualification for service as vice president."

Carnahan died in a plane crash two weeks ago while campaigning for the U.S. Senate seat held by his Republican opponent, John Ashcroft. Carnahan has surged in the polls ever since the tragedy. His rising star is the sensation of the fall political season, and already there is talk of a Carnahan challenge to Hillary Clinton in the 2004 race for the Democratic presidential nomination.

Republican leaders, however, stormed the airwaves yesterday, arguing that the dead cannot legally serve in the U.S. Senate or in any other major political position in America. Democrats countered with the example of Senator Strom Thurmond (R.-S.C.)

In an unusual twist, Carnahan, like Lieberman, is allowed under Senate rules to seek the vice presidency even while he continues his quest for a posthumous seat in the Senate. Senate Majority Leader Trent Lott (R.-Miss.) derided the situation, saying, "I just don't see how a dead man can do two jobs at once." The Gore campaign said Lott's comment was "an obscene personal attack" and that the departed governor should never be underestimated.

Lieberman, the odd man out, flew to Connecticut to campaign for his Senate seat. He said, "Though disappointed, I look forward to victory on Tuesday, and to working with Mel over the next six years. I believe he will be particularly influential as we seek to reform the so-called 'death tax.' "

Ashcroft, meanwhile, is in a delicate situation. Out of respect for the Carnahan family, he suspended his campaign as soon as he learned of the tragic plane crash. With the Lazarus-like resurgence of his opponent, however, he is gearing up again, and his campaign has prepared a TV commercial showing Ashcroft jogging, lifting weights, water-skiing, playing touch football, jumping from an airplane, donating blood, making love to his spouse, panting loudly, and listening to his own heart through a stethoscope. Aides say this is not a subtle attack on Carnahan.

Nonetheless, the Ashcroft campaign team has spared no chance to remind the electorate of the unusual choice it faces. In a brief conversation with reporters, Ashcroft mentioned on seventeen separate occasions that the latest polls show the race to be a "dead heat." Aides for George W. Bush, generally confounded by the Carnahan gambit, mulled the possibility of answering the move tit for tat—possibly by dropping Dick Cheney and replacing him with Dwight Eisenhower.

"You wanna talk about dead guys, we got 'em," Bush said during a break in *Live with Regis,* where the Texas governor has been named the permanent co-host. "We got some guys on our side who are way deader than theirs. They want to go up against Lincoln? Two can play that game."

The governor's comments triggered widespread speculation that the American political scene is facing a massive invasion by nonliving individuals who previously had played a largely symbolic role. Political historians at several universities reported receiving frantic calls from both Democrats and Republicans, seeking input on who might be available. One Washington strategist who asked not to be identified said he'd been retained by the estate of Woodrow Wilson.

In what might be merely an eerie coincidence, television stations in Southern California last night reported an empty hole, surrounded by freshly unearthed dirt, at Richard Nixon's grave site. Police said it appeared to have been exhumed from within.

The race remained incredibly close. Bush clung to a tiny lead in most national polls. Then came a stunning development on the Thursday night before the election: News organizations learned from a partisan Democrat that Bush had been arrested for drunk driving in 1976. Bush had to go in front of the cameras and admit that it was true. No one knew how any of this would play out. Would it blow over? Or would this erode Bush's already minuscule lead? And we had to wonder, were there any other bombshells out there, primed to detonate?

My mind entertained a chilling possibility.

Nov. 3

In yet another revelation that may hurt his bid for the presidency, Texas Governor George W. Bush acknowledged this morning that his 1976 arrest for drunk driving occurred while he was listening to the saccharine Swedish rock group ABBA.

"I've said all along, I made mistakes," the governor said in a hastily arranged press briefing in Kansas City. "I'm not proud of it. That night I drank too much. I got in the car and grabbed the first 8-track I saw. There was no intent, no premedication. I haven't listened to ABBA in fourteen years, and I would not buy tickets if they decided to stage a reunion tour."

A spokesman for Vice President Al Gore said today that Gore would not make any comment about Bush's atrocious musical taste.

"I think the American people can forgive the governor for a youthful indiscretion, even though this band symbolized all that was wrong with mid-1970s rock," Gore press secretary Chris Lehane said on *Good Morning America*. "But we're clearly getting into a dicey area if it turns out that he was singing along. There are serious issues here of volume. Was the sound system cranked? And what else is Bush hiding? Did he also listen to the Bee Gees? Electric Light Orchestra? Grand Funk Railroad?"

Veteran political observers were uncertain this morning whether the revelations would seriously hurt the Texas governor. It is known that neither Bush nor Gore was in peak form in 1976. Gore has acknowledged that in the 1970s he experimented with marijuana, and some observers believe that the experiment was what scientists would call "longitudinal." Gore has previously said his pot smoking was a youthful mistake, just like his book, *Earth in the Balance*. The vice president said late last night that he hadn't used marijuana in many years, except for just prior to the second debate with Bush.

"I felt I'd been too aggressive in the first debate. I admit, I got stoned to the gills. This stuff was powerful, some kind of Asian weed, one toke and you're gone. It was a bad move. I spent the whole debate thinking about whales, and the sounds they make," Gore said.

The flurry of revelations, confessions, equivocations, and temporizations began late Thursday when Fox News reported that Bush had been arrested in 1976 for driving under the influence of alcohol. Bush immediately acknowledged the accuracy of the report, but pointed out that this happened twenty-four years ago, when he was thirty years old, still living with his parents, and addicted to the primitive video game known as Pong.

He said he hadn't mentioned the arrest previously because he had wanted to set a good example for his daughters, whom he described as being extremely fragile, "like orchids." He said that, until earlier this year, he'd never informed his daughters that he was a conservative Republican.

As a parent, he said, he had no choice but to conceal his arrest record. "This wasn't some political calculation. This had nothing to do with the election," Bush said as reporters doubled over with laughter and slapped their thighs, tears pouring from their eyes and momentarily mixing with the foam that had already been forming around their mouths. So thrilled is the news media at what one network called "the developing scandal" that several reporters have indicated a complete loss of bladder control.

Bush said the judge's easy treatment of him—a small fine, a thirty-day suspension of driving privileges in Maine, and the expungement of the arrest from Bush's driving record—was not influenced by the fact that his father, at that time, was director of the Central Intelligence Agency.

"Poppy did what any concerned father with several thousand secret agents working for him would do in that situation," the governor said. "He had some guys check out the judge. Inquiries were made. The judge was shown a few surveillance photographs. All this is normal procedure."

Another startling admission came from Republican vice presidential candidate Dick Cheney. Cheney said he'd been arrested twice for drunk driving in the early 1960s. Television pundits today questioned whether Cheney was fabricating his story about being arrested, saying it might be an attempt to create a negative headline that would divert attention from Bush's latest catastrophic revelation.

Presidential historian Michael Beschloss said the situation brought to mind the bizarre 1972 incident in which Democratic vice presidential nominee Thomas Eagleton pretended to have undergone shock treatment for depression in an attempt to distract voters from presidential candidate George McGovern's communist sympathies.

Reporters scrambled this morning to find out if Bush had ever denied being arrested—for example, when filling out paperwork when seeking employment. It is routine for employers to ask job candidates if they've ever been arrested. The Bush campaign today indicated, however, that the governor had never filled out such paperwork—because this is one of the first times he's applied for a job.

Nov. 6

It's never your enemies you have to worry about. It's the people who want to help you. Your "friends."

I'm thinking, of course, of Ralph Nader. Nader is motivated entirely by the desire to help people. He wants to help the poor, the disenfranchised, the union workers. He wants to help women, minorities, gays, and lesbians. He wants to help the environment, the family farmers, the small shopkeepers. What will be the end result of all this helping? Well, he may help George W. Bush become president.

Which suits Nader fine! This is the magic of the man—the ability to see the larger picture, in which the difference between the Republicans and the Democrats is a rounding error. Never mind that Al Gore favors the McCain-Feingold campaign finance reform bill and Bush doesn't. Never mind that Bush would drill in the Arctic for oil and Gore wouldn't. Never mind that on many issues, from school vouchers to union rights to abortion rights, Gore agrees with Nader and Bush doesn't. The problem is, Gore isn't a true believer.

Gore is a sometimes-liberal. Gore compromises. Gore cuts deals. Gore is fickle. Gore zigs right and zags left. Gore is, in short, a politician. At his best, that means he has tried to be a leader and not merely a heckler. To Nader, this means Gore's a sellout, a corporate bootlicker like the rest of them. In Nader's world, your soul can't be partially saved. It's Heaven or Hell.

Back in May, on *Meet the Press*, Tim Russert asked Nader if it would bother him if he cost Gore the election (I'm taking this right from Nader's Web site). Nader answered: "No, not at all." He said a moment later, "There may be a cold shower for four years that would help the Democratic Party."

See, he's even helping the Democrats—by helping them lose.

Radicals tend to lack intellectual humility. The fuel of their crusades is their certainty, the fact that they know they're right and can't understand why others fail to agree. They flirt with millennialism, with apocalyptic scenarios. The world is a terrible mess and it may get catastrophically worse at any moment. Radicals aren't what geologists would call "uniformitarians." They would not erode the mountains gradually, they would dynamite them. Their biggest enemies are their sympathetic friends who fail to follow the hard line. In a crusade, the first order of business is to kill all the compromisers.

At his rally yesterday in Washington, Nader said that if you pick the "lesser of two evils," at the end of the day "you're still left with evil." That sums up Nader's campaign. Just about everyone in America with any power is evil, and these are particularly evil times. Many of us don't realize how bad we have it, how thoroughly infected with evil are our sorry, corrupted lives. Modern

America is virtually a sham. Bad guys run everything. Some aren't evil, perhaps, but they're evil-ish. This, at least, is my impression of what Nader is saying.

(This was a big weekend for evil. Speaking at a prayer breakfast, Gore said, "I am taught that good overcomes evil, if we choose that outcome." It was unclear if, by "evil," he meant George W. Bush specifically or the entire Republican Party. To my knowledge, Bush did not directly mention evil this weekend. That may mean he endorses it.)

There may be moments when, listening to Nader, you realize he's on to something, that he's striking a powerful chord. Sure, he's a tad argumentative, and you'd wish his Green Party would invest in a comb, but Nader talks about things that the other folks won't mention. He correctly discerns that the challenge of America is to reap the benefits of a booming technological society while minimizing the environmental damage, economic inequality, and cultural dislocations that seem to go with it. He's right, even in good times there is ugliness out there. Yes, America is too commercialized. It's awful that everything's for sale, including political parties. You'll stare at Nader in such moments and see a glow around the man, a radiance of courage and intellectual zeal.

And then suddenly, out of the blue, he'll start railing about industrial hemp. What's that about? Why are the Naderites cheering? This is clearly one of their favorite battle cries. We must legalize industrial hemp! Nader makes the point that such hemp won't get anyone high, that only the insanity of the War on Drugs has banished it from American agriculture. But would these people cheer for wheat if it was in the same position? For soybeans?

Nader has his friends. He's got Cornel West, who showed up yesterday and thanked "Comrade Nader," as though they were members of a socialist cell. The Nader candidacy, West said, was part of a much larger movement, connected to babies in Iraq, to Kurds in Turkey, and to Palestinians being killed by the "Israeli occupying army." This is one problem with the Nader coalition: A vote for Nader has a lot of fine print that you might not have noticed originally.

Recently the documentary filmmaker Michael Moore sent an open letter to Gore. After some initial wisecracks, it devolved into a rant, a three-alarm screed:

"If we ever lose *Roe v. Wade,* YOU are the one with the blood on your hands, and those of us, including Ralph Nader, who fought the Scalia nomination, will never forget the jeopardy you and your fellow Democrats put women in with that vote."

For the record, the Scalia vote was 98–0. This is because in the real world—the one that shocks and appalls Nader and his friends—the Senate usually consents to a president's choice, and does not turn every Supreme Court nomination into a Robert Bork–level partisan war.

Moore has said (and again this comes from Nader's site), "A vote for Nader is a political Molotov that we need to throw into a corrupt and bankrupt system filled with its dirty money."

Well said. Nader is a tossed grenade. People who would seek to effect change with electoral bombs have the right to do so. But bombs sometimes blow up in your hands.

Election Day. I voted, then went downtown to file by noon. The exit polls wouldn't come in until 2:00 P.M. I needed to write something that could hold up for a few hours before the returns rolled in.

Concession Speeches, November 7, 2000.
Note: All transcripts preliminary and possibly fictional.

THE VICE PRESIDENT:

I have placed a call to my opponent, Governor Bush, and have congratulated him on his victory. I wished him luck in his presidency, and apologized for any insinuations on my part, during the campaign, that he was unintelligent. Actually I did not use the word "insinuations." Throughout the phone call I refrained from using multisyllabic words. I have also placed calls of congratulations to Senator Lott, to Speaker Hastert, and to Secret Republican Lord of Darkness DeLay. When I have the time I plan to make additional calls of congratulations to the richest 1 percent of Americans.

I had hoped tonight to stand before you as the future forty-third president of the United States of America. It was a job I had prepared for since the age of two, when I first learned to deny that I needed a diaper change. I accept full responsibility for this defeat, and cast no blame whatsoever on the strategists who told me to run as an enraged, spittle-spewing populist.

Nor should this loss be attributed in any way to my association with the president, whose deplorable conduct and subsequent impeachment stood out on the political landscape as a heaving volcano of slime. The president is my friend, and although I did not want to campaign in person with him, and tried to keep him at least two time zones away at all times, I was pleased by his recent efforts to rally the vote for me in American Samoa.

I made mistakes in this campaign. First and foremost, I should have tried harder to resemble a normal human being. Since childhood I have spoken in complete paragraphs, carefully enunciated, with a slight note of condescension, even in those moments when I've slammed my thumb with a hammer. I don't even sigh normally. I sigh as though I've been practicing my sighs and try to do it too perfectly. In terms of posture, I have rigidity issues. I am the least funky man in America.

On the plus side, this defeat means that, tonight, I won't have to dance.

I know there are people who say that I pandered. To those of you who think I tried to be all things to all people, you're absolutely correct. I'm sorry for that. It was wrong. To those of you who think I did not try to be all things to all people, I think you're right, too. Thanks for your support!

There were times during this campaign when I was not certain of what kind of candidate I wanted to be. It may have been a mistake to spend the month of May, for example, campaigning as a blond. Eventually, I hit my stride and found my voice. I caught fire! Unfortunately, this happened at four o'clock this morning at the rally in Tampa.

To the American people, let me say, this election was not about Al Gore. This election was not about George W. Bush. This election was about YOU. And you have let me down. You were given the choice between good and evil. I accept your decision. This is a free country, and you are within your rights to choose the path to eternal damnation in the burning lake of fire. I would use harsher language but I'm trying to keep this on a dignified plane.

I look forward now to some downtime. Tipper and I will take a vacation and will engage in frenetic marathons of passionate love-making. If you see enormous flocks of birds exploding from the trees you'll know we're nearby. Then I will go home, as soon as I determine whether that home is in Washington or Tennessee. On the job front, I'm obviously entertaining offers. To potential employers, let me remind you: I'll do anything.

GOVERNOR GEORGE W. BUSH:

Well. What can I say? It's a shocker. Thought we had it in the bag. Had that sucker on cruise control, thought we'd kick a little Gore butt today.

I'll be straight with you, I was looking forward to the presidency. Making important decisions. Cutting taxes. Long weekends at Camp David, playing thirty-six at Burning Tree. The big plane, the helicopters, parties galore. Dad could pop in to help with the foreign stuff, like Saddam. Woulda been great!

Let me say this about the vice president: He ran a tough campaign. No hard feelings on this end. Not gonna take any POTshots.

Of course on our side we don't give out cigarettes to HOMELESS folks so they'll vote. Talk about a bunch of cheaters. Take money from the BUDDHISTS, the CHINESE, they probably got a bunch of DEAD PEOPLE in Chicago casting ballots. Trust me, we got lawyers all over this like flies on a cowpie!

And then there's this electoral college thing. Who ever heard of THAT? Totally bogus if you ask me.

I'm proud to have run a campaign based on the Republican principles of compassionate conservatism. I believe parents need to love their kids. If I'm elected president, we'll leave no child be— . . . Well, jeez, I guess I don't have to say that anymore. Phew! That 'bout drove me BANANAS.

Hell's bells, folks, let's call it a night.

RALPH NADER:

Although we did not reach the 5 percent threshold we hoped for, I think we proved that these elections are dominated by an unholy alliance of Big Business, the oil lobby, the automobile industry, the corporate media, and various secret agencies and powerful interests who do not grasp that there is a progressive movement sweeping across America that is committed to turning this great nation into something that more closely resembles a few select neighborhoods near the campus in Berkeley.

JOEL ACHENBACH:

I am sorry that the column has enraged the Left, the Right, the Far Right, and the So Far Right It's No Longer on the Spectrum. I am sorry that the column has often indulged in "humor" that was not actually funny. That is always bad, for technical reasons.

I am sorry that, back in January, I predicted a 5-to-8-point Gore victory and forgot to mention that this was something random that I typed on a whim after having too much coffee.

I am sorry that I forgot to pay more attention to obscure House races in boring states like Oklahoma.

PART FOUR

RECOUNT

THE ELECTION FROM THE BLACK LAGOON

The first batch of exit polls came in about 2:00 P.M. Tuesday. We studied them raptly. This, in all probability, would be the moment when we'd know the identity of the next president. But what we saw was rather astounding. One state after another was too close to call. I did a quick estimate of how the race was shaping up, giving every state to either Bush or Gore, a wild guess in some cases. I totaled the electoral votes. The result was going to be . . . a tie?

I had to triple-check my figures. It was true: My estimate showed 269 electoral votes for Gore and 269 electoral votes for Bush.

That night I hit the party circuit. At about 7:50 P.M., at the Lucky Bar on Connecticut Avenue, the Democrats began screaming ecstatically. The networks had called Florida for Gore. "It's over!" shouted one of the partisans. The consensus everywhere had been that if Gore won Florida and Pennsylvania and Michigan he'd be president. The networks said he'd just won the trifecta.

I checked in on euphoric Democrats partying at the Mayflower Hotel. They were stoked with confidence. I wandered over to the Capital Hilton to visit the gloomy Republicans. They were staring forlornly at a TV screen, where Bush was looking grim but defiant. Bush said his people were seeing something different in Florida. They weren't going to concede the state. As he spoke, something quite subtle happened in the corner of the screen: Gore's running electoral vote count, which had been steadily building, abruptly got smaller. It happened without any announcement. The number had just dropped by . . . twenty-five electoral votes. Florida. It had to be Florida. A minute later the news was official: The networks were all pulling back on the Florida projection. The Republicans inside the Hilton went berserk. Bush was alive!

I stuck with the Republicans until 2:20 A.M., when the networks finally called the election for Bush. The place exploded again. Dancing, victory cigars, speeches. I headed home. Finally, the election was over.

At 4:00 A.M. I checked the TV one last time. Tom Brokaw and Tim Russert were looking dazed and confused. Florida was off the board again.

In the morning I tried to write something completely outlandish. It would be based around the crazy notion that individual ballots in Florida would have to be scrutinized to see if they showed votes for Bush or Gore. Or was that just so ridiculous that it wouldn't even work as satire?

Nov. 8

Transcript of the First Presidential Ballot Counting Session:

JIM LEHRER (MODERATOR): Good evening from the Miami Beach Convention Center. I'm Jim Lehrer of the *NewsHour* on PBS. On this stage tonight I am joined by the two major presidential candidates, Vice President Al Gore and Texas Governor George W. Bush, and by these seventeen plastic bins of Florida election ballots.

An eighteenth bin, containing 3,472 ballots, has been disallowed due to the discovery that every ballot was signed with the name "Hyram J. Spinkster." Still under discussion is whether to count a large sack of ballots that mysteriously descended by parachute this morning over the city of West Palm Beach. Both campaigns have agreed that any absentee ballots cast by a citizen who then expired prior to Election Day will be counted as one half of a vote.

Under the rules established by the Emergency Presidential Commission on Counting, each candidate will be given ninety seconds to count ballots, at which time his opponent will be given thirty seconds for rebuttal. Each candidate has scratch paper and two sharpened pencils.

I alone control the pencil sharpener.

When all the ballots are counted, I will review the tabulations. The candidate with the fewest votes must bring me his tribal torch. I will then extinguish the torch and send him into the Everglades. The winner receives the presidency and one million dollars. We begin with Vice President Gore.

GORE: Thank you, Jim. Before I begin counting, I would like to remind the American people that my opponent has promised one trillion dollars of Social Security money to two different groups of people. Now, I can add one and one. One and one is two. I invite the American people to double-check my math on that. My opponent seems to disagree on this very important point, and I invite him to share with the American people his own perverse theory of mathematics. I would also—

BUSH: Stop campaigning! You know you lost! Just once say the words, "President George Walker Bush."

GORE: I won. I won the popular vote. I am more popular than you are and I'm not conceding until you admit it.

BUSH: Crybaby. Loser. *Loooooooozzzeeerrrrr.*

LEHRER: Gentlemen, this is all contrary to the rules. Mr. Vice President, please commence with the counting.

GORE: All right. Here's a Gore. Here's a Gore. That's two Gores. Here's one that's not clearly marked. Here's a—

BUSH: Not clearly marked? Jim! He's cheating already. Let me see that ballot.

GORE: You don't have to be so snippy. Look for yourself. There's just a sort of . . . blemish on the paper. A very minor indentation. There ought to be a little square hole from the ballot puncher.

BUSH: That's a hole! That's a—

GORE: That's not a hole. There's no penetration of the fiber. I don't think there's a controlling legal authority that can determine in the affirmative or negative whether that's truly a hole.

LEHRER: Gentlemen, let's put that in the "indeterminate" pile, and proceed.

GORE: Here's a Gore. Another Gore. And here's one that has something written on it. It just says, "I've fallen and I can't get up." That's clearly a Gore. That's code for "Gore."

BUSH: I help people who fall down, too! I believe in compassion for people who can't get up.

LEHRER: Indeterminate. Governor Bush, you have thirty seconds for a rebuttal, and then it is your turn to count.

BUSH: Well, look. He's a cheater. Couldn't be more obvious. This election's over. Networks called it, then they get nervous, the liberal media, can't stand to see their boy lose. You know this bozo called me on the phone and conceded, gave it up, admitted he lost, then an hour later he calls back, says he had his fingers crossed the whole time. Well, I had my fingers crossed, too, and that *cancels* his crossed-finger lie. So he's lost.

GORE: That was before I was told about the absentee ballots of soldiers stationed in Antarctica. My people say Antarctica is a Democratic stronghold.

BUSH: Give me those damn ballots.

GORE: He's grabbing!

LEHRER: Governor Bush, I think if you ask politely he will hand them over.

BUSH: All right then. Bush. Gore. Bush. Gore. Gore. Bush, another Bush. One for the jerk. Another Bush. One for the liar. One for the big dork who invented the Internet. Bush. Bush. Hah! What's that, a bunch for me already. Bush! Lookie here.

Bush everywhere. I think I'm opening up a big can of whup-ass here, Jim!

GORE: Excuse me, but I don't think such language is presidential.

BUSH: Nine for me, ten for me, six for you. Eleven for me. See I can go up higher than most people think. *Twelve* for me. *Thirteen*. Um, Jim, didn't you say we'd get calculators?

LEHRER: That was not stipulated in the rules. Mr. Vice President, you have thirty seconds.

GORE: Jim, if you look closely you will see that he is counting many of those ballots twice. Watch his hands. This is precisely like his Social Security plan and echoes all too strikingly his propensity for you-know-what—fuzzy math.

BUSH: Look, I have advisers I trust. I have good people around me. Dick Cheney is incredible with addition and subtraction. He's memorized the entire multiplication table, including the nines.

VOICE IN BACKGROUND: On behalf of the Green Party and my 96,000 Florida supporters and of all people who care about democracy and the rights of the ordinary citizen in an age dominated by craven politicians in the thrall of their corporate paymasters I—

LEHRER: Will the security guards please escort Mr. Nader to the exit.

GORE: Let me just interject that Mr. Nader will not be getting a Christmas card from the Gore family.

LEHRER: I'm afraid we are out of time and must continue with the process tomorrow night and for additional nights thereafter until we get this settled, even if that means that Campaign 2000 turns into Campaign 2001. Good night from Miami Beach.

Nov. 10

This incredible moment in American history is generating a great deal of panicky, ill-conceived, and ridiculous political punditry. I'd like to join in.

1. Al Gore will back down. He'll wait for the final vote tally before conceding, of course, but he'll abandon the Total War strategy. Thursday's press conference by the Gore lieutenants in Florida was nothing short of terrifying. By definition, you can't solve a problem, any problem, by sending a planeload of lawyers to Florida to start filing lawsuits. The typical Florida judge runs for reelection with the campaign slogan "Not Indicted Yet."

Some of Gore's friends are suggesting that it might be time to call off the dogs. They'll point out that the muddled result in this election means that Gore might be, at this moment, in the early days of his next presidential campaign. If Gore officially loses the election but wins the popular vote, he has the right to expect a Do-Over. A gracious speech now may pay off down the road. Remember this phrase: Gore in Oh-Four.

Until Tuesday night, there seemed to be only two possible futures for Gore. One was that he would be president of the United States, the most powerful man on earth, commander-in-chief of the world's most powerful military, chief executive of a vast federal administration, host of fabulous state dinners, and resident of a really swank house with its own private bowling alley. The other was that of Loser. This had appeared to be the more probable destiny.

"Loser" has typically been a full-time job for people who've run for the presidency unsuccessfully. Think of Michael Dukakis. No one has seen the man in years. I think he now plays piano in the lounge of the Holiday Inn in Reno. Last I checked, Walter Mondale was in exile in Japan, and Bob Dole famously crusades against erectile dysfunction. Many of us have fond feelings for George McGovern, but I'm pretty sure I saw him bagging groceries down at Safeway.

Gore, still in his early fifties, was poised to be a Loser on a historic scale, what with his perceived advantages as an incumbent during an economic boom. The long knives were out, ready to carve him up. But then this strange thing happened. Gore *beat* Bush.

As it stands at the moment (and this could change in the final accounting), Gore not only won the popular vote, he also narrowly won the hearts and minds of Floridians and should have gotten the state's twenty-five electoral votes. Unfortunately, there is this technicality known as "voting," and a vote is not the same thing as an opinion or an intention. It is a physical act—one that, alas, flummoxed thousands of people staring at the ballot in Palm Beach County.

(Note: I'm trying to be very careful how I word this, since in an hour I may have to retract everything. The hand count in four Florida counties and the tally of overseas ballots still could put Gore over the top. Remember, everything I say is just a "projection," based on a small statistical sample of the things I'm really thinking.)

I feel bad for Gore. He's wanted this job his entire life. You can picture him as a small boy, growing up in the Fairfax Hotel, playing with his imaginary spin doctor. No one ever ran harder for the presidency. But now he should be a patriot and go off and write a book on nanotechnology or quantum computing or cosmic evolution or some such topic that has nothing to do with presidential politics.

2. Let's obliterate this silly and, indeed, slightly snippy notion that a razor-thin Bush victory will weaken him as president. The slim Republican victories in the House and Senate will make it hard for Bush to advance his agenda, but he himself will be fully presidential.

Last night on TV the talking heads were saying that Bush would need to make some "gesture" to acknowledge that he's becoming a sort-of president. Perhaps he will have to put Democrats in his cabinet. Perhaps he will vow to spend the first three months in office doing nothing at all, just moping around the Oval Office and staring wistfully out the window. He'll still ride on *Air Force One,* but only in coach class.

In reality, the presidency is inherently transformational—it is an imperial office that exaggerates the power of its occupant. This is a job in which you can't walk from your house to your car without a military band blaring a tune. The president, simply by being the object of obsessive media scrutiny, has propaganda powers beyond those of anyone in the history of the planet. We in the media will *make* him fully presidential, even as we take potshots at him and try to prove he's a dimwit.

3. This election is like a jobs program for conspiracy theorists. The Kennedy assassination has been fairly stale for a while, and many of those folks were forced to default to the UFO invasion. Now they've got this epistemological nightmare to play with. The hard-core researchers will be examining ballots for years. Where was the CIA in all this? The anti-Castro activists? Fidel? Where in Palm Beach County can you find a grassy knoll?

I'm already preparing a rebuttal of the Single Ballot Theory.

On the weekend after the election, people started talking about the technical elements of voting, the actual mechanisms, and what happens to a ballot when it's poked with a stylus. We heard a new word: "chad."

Nov. 13

Throughout the twenty-three years I've been publisher, editor, sales manager, staff writer, and cartoonist of *Chad Watch* I've tried to warn my fellow citizens that our entire political system was vulnerable to the time bomb we call a "chad."

To say that I've been completely ignored and, indeed, treated as though I have severe hygiene problems would grossly understate the situation. Our circulation has languished in the high single figures. People I once counted as friends have derided my work as bizarre and obsessive. The mainstream news media have paid no heed to *Chad Watch*'s truly groundbreaking seventy-seven part series on the difference between a winking and blinking chad.

My parents urged me to go to law school, and several times threatened to evict me from the attic, which is not only my residence but also the *Chad Watch* newsroom. My only companion throughout these difficult years has been my pet turtle, whose name you could probably guess (rhymes with mad). It has crossed my mind that my work on chad (amazingly, some people don't realize that the plural is the same as the singular, just like "shad") has a causal relationship to my marital status (extremely single). Recently I have been forced to adopt a policy: On a first date I suppress any mention of chad until we've both ordered the main course. (Is all this too personal?)

Yes, it's been a lonely crusade. Imagine, then, my consternation—my profound shock—at the sudden national interest in chad, and particularly at the profusion of alleged "expert" commentary by Johnny-come-lately pundits who wouldn't know a flopping chad from a tumescent chad. When I see someone like pretty-boy George Stephanopoulos talking about "hanging chad" on TV it makes me want to hurl.

I will attempt to squelch such personal sentiments, however, and focus on the grave situation that has cast the presidential election in doubt. The future of our nation may hinge—pun intended!—on a few dangling chad in Florida. The current crisis over the Florida recount is by far the biggest chad story since the incredible 1993 chad-glueing scandal in the Fargo sanitation and sewer board runoff election.

The Florida debacle should give chad, and the whole chad analysis industry, the attention it has long deserved. I'm particularly heartened by the announcement this morning by Warren Christopher that the Gore campaign has a new slogan: "We Must Leave No Chad Behind."

More problematic is the declaration by the Florida secretary of state, Katherine Harris, that the 5:00 P.M. Tuesday deadline for recounting votes will be strictly enforced. This could incite a frenzy of hand-counting in the coming hours, and my fear is that the chad analysis will be superficial. We have a saying around here: "You can't rush a chad." I once spent fifteen hours studying what I thought was a two-cornered chad (or "bi-chad") but which, under closer examination with a scanning electron microscope on loan from the NASA moon rocks laboratory, turned out to be a tri-chad with associated fibroids.

What many of the so-called experts fail to grasp is that chad are a dynamic phenomenon. Consider the fact that the machines originally gave Bush a 1,700 vote lead. A recount, also by machines, whittled that lead to 327 votes. How did Gore pick up so many extra votes? Through de-chadification by partisan Democrats, of course. They didn't just handle the ballots, they stroked them, folded them, spindled them, waved them in the air, stomped them underfoot, and hung them on clotheslines until the chad became detached and a "Gore" vote could be detected by the machines.

It is likely that partisan Republicans tried to do the same thing with potential "Bush" votes, but the Democrats had an advantage: bobby pins. The bobby pin is the perfect instrument for poking a chad. Women who use bobby pins in their hair are preferentially Democratic. Republican women favor barrettes, headbands, and hair that appears to have been shellacked.

It's been reported that officials in Palm Beach County are not counting ballots with "pregnant" chad. This raises the obvious question: How pregnant? At *Chad Watch* we have long called for nationally recognized standards for describing pregnant chad according to the number of "weeks" of pregnancy, with twenty-four weeks as the threshold of viability.

Meanwhile, the reference to dimpled chad begs the question of when, exactly, we will hear of the fate of pimpled chad, knobby chad, knurled chad, mangled chad, mushed chad, pyramidical chad, poofy chad, and the legendarily problematic hairy chad.

In Palm Beach County, officials could not decide this weekend whether to apply the so-called "sunlight standard" to chad. This is when a ballot is held up to see if light passes through an alleged hole. The problem, as we've editorialized repeatedly over the years, is that the sunlight standard takes no account of meteorological variables—specifically cloud cover. A ballot that meets the sunlight standard on a sunny day is invariably rejected when there's fog.

This is an emotional moment for our country, but it can also be a teachable one. In the past week we have learned that the fate of our nation literally "hangs in the ballot" (this phrase ©*Chad Watch,* November 13, 2000. All Rights Reserved), in the form of a tiny scrap of semidetached paper.

As long as we use mechanical devices, unreliable hole punchers, and overpulped paper in our balloting system, there will be uncertainty built into the molecular structure of our democracy.

Recall that in August we learned that the conventions, despite our efforts, did not attract huge masses of people to the Internet. A scripted gathering of politicians wasn't sufficiently interesting to compel people to click repeatedly on an Internet news site. But now this happened. My readership ballooned, and I didn't even have to write irresponsible columns to rile the far right. This was the Internet story we'd been waiting for.

I flew to West Palm Beach, got a cup of café con leche at a bakery near the airport, and dove into a glorious mess.

West Palm Beach, Florida
Nov. 15

The Emergency Operations Center is out on Military Trail, an ugly strip of car dealerships, fast food joints, discount stores, and topless bars. The skyline consists of a microwave tower and lots of power lines. The EOC is bordered by a murky canal and surrounded by the kind of undersized, sun-blasted landscaping you see all over South Florida. There are reminders everywhere that this part of the world was thrown together on the fly in the last five minutes.

So many news crews are here that the county canvassing board has been holding its meetings on a flatbed trailer in the parking lot. The fact that these meetings have been beamed live to the rest of the world is the final proof of the truism that all politics is local.

This morning's session was a classic. A Republican lawyer petitioned the canvassing board to remove its most vocal, feisty member, Carol Roberts, a Gore supporter. The Republican lawyer gravely accused Roberts of counting a ballot as a Gore vote even though it didn't have a "hanging chad." Moreover, "She's been observed twisting, bending, poking, and purposely manipulating ballots."

A Democratic lawyer quickly assailed the allegation as "the most ridiculous, frivolous attack I've ever seen." The chairman of the canvassing board, Charles Burton, sought guidance from the county attorney, Denise Dytrych, who coolly informed him that, under the law, the board had no authority to remove one of its members. Burton seemed relieved. The motion did not have to be entertained at all—a simple solution. The board could return to the other, perplexing business at hand, namely trying to decide whether it could or could not start hand-counting more than 400,000 ballots.

All this was dutifully carried by cable news networks. At one point everything ground to a halt while the county attorney talked to someone on a cell phone. She covered her mouth, lest lip-readers around the world decipher her private conversation.

The unfolding story here is the precise opposite of those scripted, overhyped political conventions thrown by the Republicans and Democrats this summer. Here, no one has the slightest idea what will happen next, who'll call the shots, which votes will count, whether the dimpled or pregnant chads will pass muster, and, not incidentally, who will be the next president of the United

States. Florida has been hammered by a Category 5 hurricane of uncertainty.

There is much talk of a revote. Lots of people think they were disenfranchised the first time around. Not far from the EOC, the manager of a car dealership, Duane Mills, an African-American, said the situation was a "disaster." It brought back memories of the civil rights era. The location of the controversy was no accident. "Everything started in the Deep South, and here we are again, in the Deep South. Think about slavery, and freedom, and this and that—it was the South against the North. Now they're saying, 'You can wait four more years to vote.' "

The law is obscure, the legal rulings ambiguous. Befuddled officials turn for guidance to the top lawyers in the state and get conflicting advice. It goes without saying that everyone has a conflict of interest. Six judges yesterday recused themselves from hearing a lawsuit in Palm Beach County. Finally, Judge Jorge LaBarga heard the case. He did nothing to hide his consternation at being in the center of the presidential maelstrom. He was endearingly distressed. At one point he found himself talking to a Bush lawyer by speakerphone. All this had happened so fast, some of the lawyers had to phone in their arguments. LaBarga said to the disembodied lawyer, "How do you respond?" and then quickly added, "I know you're not prepared for this—now you know how I feel."

The Florida secretary of state, whose job is so unimportant it will be phased out in a couple of years, has become the most famous minor public official on earth. The Hollywood people surely appreciate that she is a striking, glossy, ambitious brunette who is the granddaughter of the legendary citrus baron Ben Hill Griffin Jr. It's as though the stage director shouted, "Bring on the dragon lady!"

The Palm Beach County canvassing board is intriguing precisely because of its intrinsic obscurity. Normally in America we see politics at its most glamorous, with presidential candidates and senators and powerful congressmen debating multibillion-dollar programs and weighing our relationship with China. Most politics, however, is small-scale, local, close to the ground. It's about zoning variances. It's about firefighter pension plans. It's about buying a couple of new garbage trucks. It's a process driven by gadflies, county commissioners, state legislators, and other folks who will never attend a state dinner at the White House.

And now, for a few moments, they have their day in the sun.

The canvassing board meetings in the parking lot have a certain structure and pattern. Presiding is Burton, a heavy-faced judge who does not hide his frustrations and does not seem to relish his sudden celebrity. To his right, Theresa LePore, the elections supervisor whose design of the Palm Beach County ballot may have changed American history, remains mute and withdrawn behind dark sunglasses. Associates say she is depressed, feeling battered by former friends who've attacked her on TV and won't forgive her for the ballot fiasco. To Burton's left is Roberts, the driving force in the effort to recount manually the Palm Beach votes. Sometimes the partisans show up to lend some background noise. Tuesday afternoon the Gore people chanted "Every vote counts!" while the Bush people chanted "We won twice!"—the two chants mingling incomprehensibly, joined by the hum of nearby TV truck generators and the occasional drone of an overhead plane.

Lawyers for the two campaigns are always on hand, easily distinguished by their power broker suits and expensive haircuts. Their viewpoints are relentlessly predictable. These folks were unknown to the nation until a few days ago. As the Tuesday afternoon meeting progressed, a local reporter whispered, "These are jobs that never mattered. This canvassing board, this was a joke!"

It seems as though there have been a profusion of mega-stories in recent years, from the O.J. trial to the Lewinsky scandal to the Elian Gonzalez case. To some extent it's the result of the media apparatus itself, of the infrastructure that makes the monster story possible. But this story is different. It almost seems bigger than any of the others. This is a story with which we are completely unfamiliar. We're deep in the murk.

We have discovered there are no rules in the swamp.

I hit the road, looking for material. The route was obvious: Southern Boulevard runs the breadth of the county, from one extreme to the other, Belle Glade to Palm Beach.

In western Palm Beach County the sugarcane rises from soil so dark they call it black gold. I saw a fog to the north—ashes from burning fields. The horizon is flat but for the processing plant, belching smoke into a reddening sky. The cutting season had begun and the migrants had arrived. I stopped at Glades Truck Ice, where a cannon shoots snow onto truckloads of fresh vegetables. The crewman, Dudley Clark, a man who grew up here, served in the army, and came home, was emphatic about what should be done: "Throw away the ones they got now, throw them all out the window, and have another election. If they don't do it right, they'll always be saying, he didn't deserve to win, he cheated."

At the bowling alley next door the first customers were drifting in and the owner, Tom Cole, had just made a pot of coffee. Next to the cash register was a large vat of pickled sausages, dyed a color of red I'd never previously encountered. These sausages looked like something from outer space. In this long year of political craziness, this was possibly the most amazing thing I'd seen—especially since the vat was only half full! The rest had been eaten. Or perhaps used somehow in the act of bowling.

Cole laughed at the election mess. "It's the most ridiculous thing I've ever seen in my life. Everybody saying they were confused by the ballot? I'm sorry, if you can't follow arrows, there's something wrong."

Halfway to West Palm Beach, I stopped at Lion Country Safari. The public relations woman, L. J. Margolis, gave me a tour of the big cats, the zebras, the antelope, the rhinos, the giraffes. The gi-

raffes were looking down on us through the sunroof. One lion kept growling. I remembered that it is traditional, when writing about a presidential campaign, to end your coverage with some kind of freak, tragic encounter with a ravenous mammal. The PR woman, for her part, was not worried by rumors of a tourist boycott. The election catastrophe meant name recognition. "We're all tickled. We don't expect people to confuse us with Palm Springs, California, anymore. It really puts us on the map!"

They feel the same way, no doubt, in Chernobyl.

I kept driving. The road ends in Palm Beach proper, at Mar-a-Lago, the famed mansion of Marjorie Merriweather Post, now a private club—extremely private. The valets, to their credit, did not attempt to shoot out the tires of my approaching rental car, but neither did they see the wisdom of allowing me to enter, interview the members, use the john, and pilfer free food. Journalistic ethics, long established, required me to mock these obscenely rich and spiritually bankrupt people in my very next column.

Palm Beach
Nov. 16

Two Republicans are standing on the sidewalk on Worth Avenue, waiting for the valet to bring the Jag. They're sated and happy after a sumptuous meal at a dark restaurant with a piano player tickling the ivories in the corner. Yet they are not free of pain and suffering. The disastrous presidential election has cast aspersions on their city. They know what people are saying—those folks down in Palm Beach are idiots.

"They keep saying, 'It's Palm Beach.' But it's Palm Beach *County*, it's not Palm Beach," says Barbara Robertson. "We resent that. It gives us a bad image!"

She voted, despite her GOP leanings, for Gore. So did her husband, who declines to offer a name (although she keeps referring to him as "Harrison"). He says Gore was right on the important issues, and "the other fella's a nincompoop." Both, however, are tired of this endless, chaotic, lawsuit-entangled presidential election.

"I just want it over. We don't care now *who* gets in," she says.

The valet is standing by impatiently with the keys to the Jag.

"Barbara, your chariot awaits," the husband says.

You get a different opinion everywhere you look in this county. But everyone's getting fed up. They are unanimous in their view that this election was a historic mess. Our ship of state has sailed into the Perfect Storm.

Until November 7 we had a political technique that seemed perfectly designed for resolving a dispute about who should lead the country. It was called an "election." This time it didn't work.

Two people think they won. Both think they got the most votes. Who's right? There is no "right." This is beyond that. The nation is straining to hear the sound of one hand clapping. There are rumors that a tree fell in the forest, but there is no confirmation that it made a sound. There are limits to the knowable. You can't prove that parallel lines never meet. The silliest phrase in circulation is "the will of the people," as though this is something coherent and definite. We lack the instruments to measure this thing. The people have spoken: They want the next president to be either Bush or Gore.

Both sides think the other is trying to steal the election. (Joe Lieberman said this morning, "I would never use the word 'steal' . . ." but it was obvious that he would let the word bound around freely within his skull.) You can understand why Al Gore would want to see if he's got enough uncounted votes from "undervoted" ballots out there to make him the next president. You can also see why George W. Bush would want the counts in Democratic strongholds halted.

The Bush campaign is trying hard to make the case that Bush already is the victor. Three times in a single press conference Tuesday night, Karen Hughes, Bush's press secretary, said, "Governor

Bush won." Never mind that there are uncounted overseas ballots and that they might conceivably give the victory to Gore.

"You win when you're ahead at a stopping point. We were ahead at a stopping point," explained Tucker Eskew, a spokesman for the Bush campaign, as he waited for the latest announcement from the county canvassing board. He compared it to the World Series. You can "win" games before you've won the Series.

While Palm Beach County officials tied themselves in knots trying to decide if a recount would be legal, Broward County officials dove into recounts with both hands. To the list of the names of previously obscure local officials now on global television, we add "Judge Robert Lee" and "Suzanne Gunzburger," the two Democrats on the Broward canvassing board. Republicans are screaming that the heavy-handed Broward counters are detaching those accursed chads. Chads are flying everywhere! One Republican activist this morning called it "Hurricane Chad."

The Broward hand count is proceeding despite the announcement from the secretary of state, Katherine Harris, that she will ignore any new numbers from Broward. In a few days she will certify the final numbers and pay no heed to anyone running around with a fistful of Gore votes. Harris last night assured the nation that her decision to exclude any consideration of further vote counts was reached "independently," which presumably means that it was not influenced in the slightest by the fact that she is co-chair of the Bush campaign in Florida.

Let's keep this issue of "bias" in perspective: She's labored for a year for a Bush victory and has well-known ambitions for an ambassadorship to an exotic foreign country, such as Brazil, under a Bush administration, and would like to be the next Republican senator from Florida, but it's not like she's an immediate *blood relative* of the guy.

Bulletin: This morning Governor Jeb Bush vouched for Harris's objectivity.

Plantation, Florida
Nov. 17

No one was prepared for the immaculate chad. It was a chad that scoffed at the laws of probability. It was not an ordinary chad, not merely pregnant, dimpled, hanging or dangling. It had no visible detachment from the ballot. It was, rather, *reversed*. It was occupying the number 3 hole, the Gore hole, but the little black dot that should have been on the front side was, incredibly, on the back. It was a fully flopped-over, inverted, reciprocal, miracle chad.

Conclusion: A rogue, foot-loose chad had plugged the hole.

"Evidently, it floated in there somehow," said the Broward county supervisor of elections, Jane Carroll.

One more vote for Gore. Republican lawyers, observing closely, disapproved vehemently.

"It shows this process is flawed. How do they know the ballot wasn't printed incorrectly?" said Republican party official George Lemieux.

Ah, but there was one other bit of data about this particular ballot, and the canvassing board found it compelling: A machine had already recorded the ballot as a Gore vote. There had been a hole in the ballot in Gore's spot. Presumably it was only after that point that the immaculate chad came swooping in.

You can see that the pressure of the moment has created a rather surreal atmosphere here at the Emergency Operations Center, a modern concrete fortress parked on 84th Avenue in the congested Broward suburbs. Nothing is trivial in this high-stakes game. The situation is simultaneously historic and hysterical. Lawyers are swarming. Subpoenas cloud the air like gnats. The Republicans, alert for fraud, have demanded that all surveillance tapes of the vote-counting room be preserved.

The Republicans show a particular interest in the chads.

Thursday night the Republicans got on their hands and knees and gathered up the tiny scraps of paper from the floor. "No fair observer can dispute that there are extraordinary irregularities going on in this recount," said Ed McNally, a lawyer and Bush campaign volunteer. "I think the fact that Broward County sheriff's deputies seized seventy-eight chads last night utterly confirms that the massive handling and rehandling of these ballots is degrading them physically." He brandished a photograph showing a sheriff's deputy sorting the chads into clusters of five.

The chads were then placed in a manila envelope. According to the Associated Press, someone helpfully put a label on the envelope: "Crime. Found Property." The sheriff's office, however, says it is not conducting an investigation.

The task in Broward is formidable. Hundreds of people are manually recounting 588,000 ballots. Jane Carroll says she has seen nothing like it in her thirty-two years as elections supervisor, and frankly she's not happy about it. She looks around the room and sees unfamiliar faces. She likes to keep things under tight control, and this is slow-motion mayhem. "I like organization," she says.

By Thursday night, Gore had a net gain of twenty-one votes with ninety out of 606 precincts counted. But it might be garbage data: Florida Secretary of State Katherine Harris says she won't heed the new numbers, and this morning a Florida judge backed her up. It looks as though the election might actually end this weekend.

Despite this morning's ruling, the Broward recount continued at full speed, which is to say, at an excruciatingly tedious pace. Every ballot is scrutinized by four people: two "counters" who work for the county, and two "observers," one Republican and one Democrat. The ballots have no words on them, just columns of numbers. The first column is the presidential race. The voter was supposed to use a metal stylus to punch a hole in the ballot at the number corresponding to the preferred candidate. The ballot has a perforated chad ready to fall out when poked. Sometimes, though, voters don't push hard enough. The chad sticks in some fashion. It might remain attached by a single corner, or two corners, or three, or it might merely be dimpled, also known as "pregnant."

The standard in Broward is relatively strict: A vote only counts if the chad is detached at two corners. A one-corner chad or a dimpled chad is a no-vote, or "undervote." Up in Palm Beach County, by contrast, a one-corner chad is counted.

If any of the four people examining the ballot has a dispute about the vote, the ballot is channeled to the canvassing board in the next room. The canvassing board is a motley group. The chairman is County Judge Robert Lee, a rather effervescent fellow who normally handles domestic violence cases. His liberal flank is occupied by County Commissioner Suzanne Gunzburger, a former teacher who seems to be relishing the chance to do something historic. On his other side is Carroll, a Republican, who cast the lone vote against the recount.

They proceed with all due deliberation. The ballots are passed back and forth gingerly, and showed to the partisan observers.

"Sixteen-N-one is a clear undervote . . . Sixteen-N-two is a clear undervote . . . Sixteen-N-three appears to me two corners attached."

"Which person?"

"Bush."

"I see what you're talking about."

"That's no different from a lot of the other ones."

"There is a net gain of one for Bush."

It does not appear to be a foolproof arrangement. Cardboard boxes of ballots keep coming into the room, and several times yesterday there were concerns that ballots had been misplaced. "We're missing two ballots," Lee announced at one point. "We need someone to recount this box." A moment later he said, "Actually, it could be one off, rather than two." The process did not reek of precision.

The board members were hit with subpoenas in the middle of the afternoon. Gunzburger said, "It could be squashed."

"Quashed," the judge said.

"It could be squashed *and* quashed," Carroll said.

Television producers are trying to line them up for interviews, but they're getting picky.

"I turned down the *Today* show, and *Good Morning America,* and I'm sure not going to do the other one," Carroll said.

At the end of the day, there's something on the floor. It's so small as to be almost invisible. But yes: It's a chad. Retrieved on a wet fingertip, it has the signature dot in the center. A historic chad! Portentous and controversial! But how would anyone know if it was a chad from the presidential race or a chad from, say, the dog-catcher race? Is there some way to distinguish the important chad from the irrelevant chad?

Jane Carroll shook her head in the negative.

"A chad is a chad," she said.

Nov. 20

There's a gaping hole, or at least a considerable dimple, in the Republican contention that the Democrats are manufacturing votes in Florida. The truth is, so far the votes in the presidential election have been systematically *undercounted*. Votes aren't being manufactured, they're being ignored.

More precisely, the canvassing boards are putting many hundreds of ballots to one side, pending further instructions, because the infamous chad isn't detached. It's merely "dimpled" or "pregnant." The Republicans, naturally, say such ballots shouldn't count. But here's a crucial point they never mention: It is essentially impossible for a chad to become pregnant accidentally. *There must be an impregnator.* That impregnator was, almost certainly, the original citizen who handled the ballot.

Some of those are votes for George W. Bush. Some are for Al Gore. Given the voting patterns in South Florida, more are probably for Gore. Here we see one reason why the Republicans can't walk two paces without letting out a panicked squeal. They don't want Gore to steal the election on the slim technicality that he got more votes. It's possible, I should note, that Gore didn't get more votes. The recounts so far haven't produced quite the bonanza of Gore votes that some people anticipated. And nearly half of the overseas absentee ballots, which favored Bush, were disqualified for technical reasons, such as the absence of a postmark. The Gore campaign circulated a memo offering lawyers advice on objecting to military ballots. Hundreds of legitimate Bush votes may not have been counted.

That said, when I was in Broward County on Friday night, the loudest objections to the absentees were from the Republican lawyers. They were in Gore country and they must have presumed that the overseas absentees wouldn't tilt in their favor. When the absentee ballot counting session was over, Gore had fifty-three votes and Bush had thirty-seven—but 246 ballots had been disqualified.

I am not naive enough to think that the candidate with the most votes should win an election. That's the kind of uninformed, romantic, antediluvian belief that I clung to until about thirteen days ago. We now know that it is the candidate with the best lawyers who should win an election.

Two lower courts ruled against manual recounts. Now the canvassing boards are waiting for the Florida Supreme Court to weigh in. In the meantime the Republicans are howling. The rules keep changing. They think they're witnessing a crime in progress. It is, to be sure, an amazing sight. The Broward County Emergency Operations Center is designed to handle natural disasters, not electoral ones. The counters can sometimes look up at the huge TV screens and see themselves counting.

I asked several of the Republican spinners to explain how, precisely, the vote counters are manufacturing votes for Gore. The spinners looked at me as though I was a moron, a Martian, or perhaps that strangest creature of all, a liberal. They all cited the circumstantial evidence of the chads. There are hundreds, thousands of them on the floor. A chad blizzard! A chad whiteout! You can't see across the room, what for the fog of chad!

Republicans claim that the constantly handling, shuffling, and buffeting of the ballots is causing them to "degrade." They're losing their "integrity." I'm patiently waiting for someone, anyone, to show me how the mere handling of a ballot without any previous punch mark for Al Gore—a ballot that is simply blank in the presidential column—will preferentially degrade it in favor of Gore.

What might happen, to be sure, is that a dangling, hanging, swinging chad might, through handling, become a fully detached chad. But why is that bad? Isn't that good? The reason the chad was dangling like that is (in all likelihood) because someone punched the ballot. Why not count it? (Note: If someone wanted to create a fraudulent vote for Gore they wouldn't leave the chad hanging or dimpled.) Republicans complain that certain people are showing up as county-employed vote counters one day, then returning as partisan Democrat observers the next. Plus you got the chad eaters. Two Democrats thought it'd be cute to eat a chad. The Republicans were unamused. ("We offered to get back the chad after this guy was through with it," said Democrat observer Steve Geller.)

Admittedly, the process isn't exactly what you'd call scientific. Ballots have been dropped and stepped on. The canvassers have resorted to magnifying glasses, like Sherlock Holmes, as they try to read faded or smudged postmarks. The canvassing board meets at a table that is forever covered with dozens of different piles of ballots, various stacks of paper, cardboard boxes, and legal pads scrawled with numbers. Jane Carroll, the elections supervisor, told me that only once before, in thirty-two years on the job, has she overseen a hand count. It was for a tiny town with one precinct.

The mayor's race had come down to a single vote. It took three hand recounts to come up with a result that seemed about right.

Here, finally, we come to solid ground in the Republican complaint. Over time this process of recounting will not necessarily reach the truth of the Florida vote. There is abundant opportunity for human error. The recount is taking place only in a few counties that lean Democratic.

If Gore prevails, millions of Americans will feel that the outcome was corrupt. It does feel a bit like the U.S.-Soviet basketball game at the 1972 Munich Olympics, when the officials kept putting time back on the clock, until finally the Soviets prevailed.

At some point the whistle has to blow.

In a shocker, the Florida Supreme Court unanimously ruled that the manual recounts in South Florida should continue and their results included in the official tally. The ruling created a firestorm. Republicans in the Florida legislature threatened to defy the Florida Supreme Court and appoint their own slate of Bush electors. Our nation's most distinguished public officials were now openly accusing each other of trying to steal the election. Elder statesmen of the Washington political scene were talking about a constitutional crisis. This was a new vibe on the American political scene, a hint of what it is like to live in countries where power does not change hands in a peaceful and orderly fashion. We could smell it: the malodorous whiff of anarchy.

Nov. 22

Emboldened by their momentous victory at the Florida Supreme Court, but fearing they still may lack the votes they need to win, strategists for Vice President Al Gore filed a lawsuit today to force elections officials to credit Gore with all 97,421 votes cast for consumer activist Ralph Nader.

"Every vote should count," said Gore adviser Warren Christopher, who with each passing day has more closely resembled one of Santa's elves. "The Nader votes were really Gore votes. Everyone knows it. We should also look more closely at votes for this person from the Natural Law Party, Mr. Hagelin, and at votes for the various socialists, the Trotskyites, all the crazy fringe people."

Election law experts say vote reassignment, as it is formally known, is a delicate procedure, requiring courts to ascertain not only the intent of the voter but also what the intent of the voter would have been had the voter not been misguided or irresponsible. Vote reassignment is rare in the United States, but has been attempted in other countries, most recently in the presidential election in Yugoslavia.

Nader, who does not own a telephone, could not be reached for comment.

The latest developments followed the dramatic decision by the Florida Supreme Court to allow hand recounts in several Florida counties. In their forty-two-page opinion, the justices declared that votes should be carefully counted by hand and the winner should be the candidate who received the most votes. It said that technicalities should not decide an election. Bush campaign strategists denounced the ruling as "insane," "hallucinatory," and "a Marxist-Leninist rant."

Texas Governor George W. Bush, sensing that the political situation is careening out of control, went on national television today to reassure the nation. He said the election is being stolen, that democracy itself is imperiled, and that Gore is a "big cheater." He said the Florida Supreme Court has no business interpreting the laws of the state. He did not explain what he believes the court's duties are supposed to be.

At the end of the brief press conference he wished Americans a pleasant Thanksgiving, despite the desecration of the Constitution. As he left the room he was overheard telling an aide that he hopes the Gore family's turkey is "overcooked and really dry."

Gore appeared on television Tuesday night, after the court ruling, to say that it does not matter who the winner of the election is, so long as it is him. He said that he continues to believe that every vote should be counted, including ballots with dimples so slight they can only be detected by theoretical physicists at leading universities. Ballots that are completely blank, he said, should be interpreted by psychics.

Attorneys for Gore, in yet another confusing twist to the situation, said they would appeal the Supreme Court ruling. When reporters pointed out that they'd won the case, the attorneys said that was legally irrelevant.

"The important thing here is that all this legal action is billable," said the lead attorney for the Democrats, David Boies, adding, "Christmas came early."

Republicans in the Florida legislature were furious about the court ruling and suggested that they may ignore it. If so, it would set up the constitutional crisis that political pundits have been claiming to fear but privately crave.

The Florida Republicans could choose to appoint a Republican slate of electors regardless of the final vote count in the state. That would set up a battle in the Senate, which has the right to contest the seating of presidential electors. Currently the Republicans have fifty seats in the Senate and the Democrats have forty-nine, with one seat, from Washington state, still undecided. If there is a 50–50 tie, the tie-breaking vote would be cast by the incumbent vice president—Al Gore. Gore promised last night that, should he be put in the position of having the deciding vote in the election, he would be "entirely objective."

"I will look carefully at Governor Bush's proposals, and at my own, and after weighing their various merits, I will decide independently—just like that Katherine Harris person down there in Florida—who will be the next president," Gore said.

Breaking News Bulletin: Several news organizations are chasing a rumor that this entire election drama is merely something that *Meet the Press* host Tim Russert is dreaming. Executives at

NBC said today that, if this is the case, they will awaken Russert as soon as the November sweeps are over.

As I filed that last column, at noon on Wednesday, the day before Thanksgiving, Gore had tremendous momentum from the Florida Supreme Court ruling. That changed 90 minutes later. Partisan Republicans from Washington had spent the morning participating in a raucous, fist-waving protest at the scene of the recounts in Miami-Dade County. At 1:30 P.M. the Miami-Dade canvassing board abruptly voted to halt the recounts, saying it couldn't finish the job by the 5:00 P.M. November 26 deadline imposed by the Florida Supreme Court. Democrats charged that the Miami-Dade officials had been intimidated by a Republican "mob." Gore was crushed; he didn't see how he could prevail without more votes from Miami.

More trouble for Gore: The Palm Beach County canvassing board members took a day off on Thanksgiving, and by midday Sunday realized that they wouldn't quite finish the recount by five in the afternoon. They asked Secretary of State Katherine Harris for a few extra hours. She refused the request. The Palm Beach canvassers busted the deadline by two hours and eight minutes. Their final tally—with a net gain of more than 200 votes for Gore—was disregarded by Harris, as were more than 160 votes for Gore found in Democratic precincts in the abortive recount in Miami-Dade.

At 7:30 P.M., Harris went before the news media and said, "I hereby declare Governor George W. Bush the winner of Florida's twenty-five electoral votes for the president of the United States." Bush, she said, had received 2,912,790 votes, and Gore 2,912,253, a margin of 537.

Bush addressed the nation two hours later, saying he was "honored and humbled to have won the state of Florida." Minutes later, Joe Lieberman went on TV with his own message: The Democrats weren't conceding. They would formally contest the election results in court.

The General Services Administration, meanwhile, refused to give Bush and Cheney the keys to the government offices set aside for the presidential transition. And there was yet another party still to be heard from: The United States Supreme Court. Bush had appealed the November 21 ruling by the Florida Supremes that had allowed the manual recounts. That ruling now seemed pretty much moot — the recounts were over and Bush remained in the lead — but the Republicans didn't know what other tricks the Florida judges might have up their sleeves. Bush, taking a gamble, pressed ahead with the federal case. Oral arguments would be later in the week.

This, then, was a typical moment in the Florida recount: The loser was going to court, as was the winner.

Nov. 27

What an awkward moment for George W. Bush. He's dreamed of being president ever since he was fifty-one years old and an aide told him that he was leading in a poll of possible Republican presidential candidates. Now, suddenly, he's got the White House practically in his grasp—but no one will give him the keys. The General Services Administration refuses to let him into his ninety-thousand-square-foot transition office. Bush is going to have to creep into town in the middle of the night and jimmy a window.

Never has a victorious presidential candidate faced so difficult a transition. Bush has to get ready to be the most powerful man on earth, but—this is critical—without appearing "presumptuous." His new status as president-elect is conditional, and he's not allowed to know what the conditions are. He is being stalked by a giant asterisk.

In his "victory" speech last night, Bush had to make sure he didn't sound triumphant. In an almost apologetic tone he mentioned that he'd been certified the winner in Florida and thus had "the needed electoral votes to win the election." Gingerly, he said he was preparing to serve as our new president. It was a bit like a prospective stepfather meeting his fiancée's child: "Suzy, it looks like I'm going to be your new Daddy."

Bush said the right things. He presented himself as the leader of all the people and not just of a single party. He talked of bipartisan goals. His disapproval of the legal tactics of Gore was stated directly but politely. He sought to be a healer, a unifier.

Unfortunately, Bush looks ten years younger every time we see him. He's regressing before our eyes. At this rate he will soon start wearing a little sailor suit with short pants. Whenever Bush has to speak in a formal manner he has a relapse into his deer-in-the-headlights look. You see a man who has been practicing this role offstage, talking to a mirror. He seems to be trying hard to walk like a president, stand like a president, and speak like a president, without making any blunders; but the cumulative effect has a certain "student council" quality.

The difficulty in appearing presidential is a problem that everybody faces in Bush's position. A candidate who wins a presidential race goes through a geeky phase of being quite incredible and even a bit ridiculous. Millions of Americans see their new leader on TV, turn to their spouse, friend, dog, or cat, and say, "I just can't *believe* this guy is supposed to be our president." Even in the year 2000, people say this about Bill Clinton.

The critics say George W. Bush fails upward, and this election will give them abundant ammunition. But such attacks are unfair to the Texas governor. Although it's true that he would be nowhere without his famous name, had an undistinguished business career, and is still the least impressive person at the dinner table when the Bush clan gets together for holidays, he did manage to go out and campaign fairly competently after the Republican nomination was handed him by party mandarins. Let's give the man credit!

His biggest problem, in terms of credibility, is that ⸏ election. Political historians will argue for decades over tᵢ degree to which Bush was beaten by Al Gore. Some maver. ing to be sensational, may go so far as to claim that Gor actually win. This peculiar situation—the loser becoming dent—has happened before in our nation's history, thoug since the advent of electricity. It is nice to know that our sc hasn't completely lost touch with the old-fashioned, ninetee century way of doing things.

(Last night Joe Lieberman said, "It is in our nation's inter that the winner in Florida is truly the person got the most votes This is the kind of utopian, touchy-feely, bleeding-heart thinkin, that got the Democrats in trouble years ago.)

There are a few legal details that have to be ironed out before this election achieves closure. Gore, for example, has not conceded. He is fighting the result in court, and may soon start campaigning once again in Iowa and New Hampshire. For the first time this year he has crowds spontaneously gathering to show support for him. They assemble outside his home, chanting "Gore Got More!" It is unfortunate for Gore that his 2000 presidential campaign did not really catch fire until late November.

Should Gore give up? Some ding-dong Internet columnist said a couple of weeks ago that Gore should back off and wait for 2004 to take revenge. But I think the public should grant Gore some time to contest the election result, in part because we don't really have anything else to do this week. My schedule's clear, I know that. For all the handwringing about what a constitutional nightmare this is, it's actually rather entertaining, strangely similar to watching sports on TV. This month, CNN and ESPN have been indistinguishable.

Gore can't win, at this point; but he can still torment Bush. He can inflict pain. He can make Bush feel like there's a Gore lawyer lurking behind every curtain, under the bed, and in the shower

stall. If Gore plays his cards right, he can force Bush to glance repeatedly in his direction during the January 20 swearing-in ceremony.

You know what Bush will be thinking when he looks at the vice president: *Keep your dadgum hands off that Bible.*

Nov. 30

Timeline on Breaking Developments in Campaign 2000:

8:15 A.M.: With TV helicopters providing live coverage, Ryder rental truck containing more than one million South Florida ballots, and driven by Joe Lieberman, sets out on the long journey to Tallahassee.

8:17 A.M.: Ryder truck rammed by Buick driven by Bob Dole.

8:35 A.M.: Dick Cheney arrives in Austin with future Secretary of State Colin Powell. They meet with George W. Bush, thank him for his efforts during the campaign, and discuss possible roles for Bush in the Cheney-Powell administration.

8:37 A.M.: Al Gore, having appeared on every major network in twenty-four hours to explain why he should be president, telephones CNN executives and asks if he can argue the "left" position on *Crossfire*. Executives say they do not have an opening until the middle of next week.

8:55 A.M.: Republican legislators in Tallahassee call a special emergency session to deal with the possibility that the election will end without any of them becoming famous.

9:07 A.M.: Attorneys for Gore, saying time is of the essence, ask a Florida circuit court judge to order an immediate recount of the recount of the recount of the original vote count, this time using a "base 4" numeric system. The judge responds with a backwoods adage involving a polecat, chewing tobacco, and a sinkhole that reporters agree is completely incomprehensible.

9:21 A.M.: Ryder truck apparently takes wrong turn at famed

"Golden Glades" interchange and begins driving south, toward Key West.

9:32 A.M.: Back in Texas, negotiations with Bush break down momentarily when Bush demands Wednesdays off.

9:44 A.M.: Al Gore appears as special guest in third hour of the *Today* show, following segment on new techniques for whisking egg whites.

10:00 A.M.: Attorneys for Gore, to save time, file appeals of "possible future rulings" by various courts in Florida. Gore attorney David Boies issues a "provisional" denunciation of unfair and unconstitutional rulings "should they occur." In West Palm Beach, more than three thousand citizens who believe they inadvertently voted for Pat Buchanan hold a rally. Hundreds are taken to the hospital with facial injuries after walking accidentally into a telephone pole.

10:22 A.M.: Bush demands his own parking space. Cheney and Powell say they can probably work something out. Bush, relieved, agrees to serve vaguely defined role as "special adviser to the vice president."

11:02 A.M.: Attorneys for Gore say that, if they lose at the U.S. Supreme Court, they will appeal the case to an international tribunal in The Hague.

12:01 P.M.: TV helicopters sight Ryder truck on a ship heading across the Florida Straits, toward Cuba.

12:50 P.M.: Tim Russert, doodling with electoral college numbers on a white slate, suddenly discovers the elusive "elegant proof" of Fermat's Last Theorem.

Dec. 1

There were oral arguments this morning at the Supreme Court, mostly in the form of chants.

"Gore got more! Gore got more!"

"Bush has won! Bush has won!"

"Racist, sexist, anti-gay, you can't take our votes away!"

"Take it like a man! Take it like a man! Take it like a man! . . ."

The crowd was divided by politics and a large number of beefy cops. The endless presidential campaign had arrived, inevitably, at the great stone temple of jurisprudence on Capitol Hill. This was no place to find a carefully nuanced position. People came to yell.

We are in a moment when approximately half the country knows with absolute certainty that the other half is wrong. At the moment it's just about the only thing we can all agree on—that (Gore/Bush—pick one) is trying to squirm and slither his way into an illegitimate presidency. In front of the Supreme Court this morning you could get completely contradictory views merely by walking a few feet.

They weren't angry so much as righteous. It is thrilling to possess a conviction about what is just, what is fair, and have the opportunity to express it on the steps of the grandest court in the land. There was no missing the note of euphoria. A thrill was in the air. This was a political space-time singularity, the right moment and the right place to register an opinion with no chads attached.

"It's like the Super Bowl for political junkies," said Nancy Banasiewicz, who got on a bus at five in the morning in Atlantic City to ride to Washington with sixty-six fellow Bush supporters.

"This is like the Boston Tea Party of twenty-first century. This is something they'll talk about forever," said Frank Williams, a New Jersey tour guide who put together the bus trip.

Joshua Lehner, a George Washington University student holding a "We Need a President Who Can Read" sign, said, "I'm just here to have fun and irritate some Republicans who watch too much CNN."

A man in a Darth Vader costume wandered around calling for the votes to be counted "until the Dark Side wins." A man held a cardboard Christmas tree with a yellow flashing light on top and the words "G.W. Bush: Dimmest Bulb on the Tree." Amid the shouts and laughter a few yellow-sweatshirted members of the

Falun Gong sect stood frozen in meditation, minds somewhere far away from these transitory passions.

Bush voter Ron Floyd, a Catholic University politics major, says Gore is hurting the nation by contesting the election: "I know I'm taking a hit in the stock market; I don't know about you."

A few steps away, Gore supporter Lovern J. Louis said of the election controversy, "I see it as an embarrassment to the nation on a global scale. We send folks to monitor elections—we send people to enforce the rules of democracy. In our own backyard, we got amnesia and forgot those same rules and principles. Fidel Castro is talking about sending people here to help us count votes. They're laughing at us!"

And now back to a Bush person: Dave McIntosh, a glassblower from Egg Harbor Township, New Jersey, said of Gore, "I think he's being ridiculous and selfish and he's dragging this nation through hell. I wish I could charge him for what it's costing me to take this day off. Give it up already!"

Perhaps the Supreme Court will settle the matter once and for all, digging through case law going back to—what?—the Magna Carta? More likely, any decision by any party, any court, any candidate, will be viewed through a partisan lens. Distrust is not easily abated. Like suspicion, it tends to fester.

Americans agree on general principles of law and order and constitutional government. There is no crumbling of the basic social compact. But neither are we on the verge of some great unification. There is talk, in the wake of the historically close election, and the neatly divided Congress, that we'll see an era of bipartisanship, of "comity," of lambs lying with the lions. But guess what? Division is more fun. Division motivates.

We like having an opponent. We like squaring off against the cheaters, the jerks, the bad guys. There are two kinds of people in the world—the kind of people who like a sharp political dispute and the kind who love it.

Dec. 6

Everyone knows about the hijinks in Seminole and Martin counties, where Republican activists "fixed" technical flaws in thousands of Republican absentee ballot applications. But that only scratches the surface of the malodorous, mephitic mire that is the Florida presidential election. Consider:

- In Stankee County, officials let Republican activists take Democratic absentee ballots to Bubba's All-Nite Meat Shak, where subsequent stains from barbecue sauce rendered the ballots unreadable.
- In Chaw County, on the Alabama border, Republican elections officials required voters in predominantly Democratic precincts to submit first to fingerprints, mug shots, frisking, and "cavity checks," while in Republican precincts every voter was given free tickets to the annual Kiwanis Club fish fry.
- In Shiffless County, Republican officials fed hundreds of Democratic ballots to a pack of starving pit bulls.
- In tiny Crawdad County, in the Florida panhandle, elections officials recorded 17,821 votes for George W. Bush even though the county's population, including livestock, is only 185.

Taken individually, these cases are certainly not a cause for alarm. Americans are sophisticated, and they understand that in some circumstances a ballot must be reviewed by partisan activists, and possibly improved, altered, destroyed, or subjected to what is known as "the multiplier effect." But as we read all the various reports, it becomes increasingly evident that our procedures for electing a president are not entirely foolproof—a problem hinted at earlier this year when the two major parties, defying common sense, nominated Al Gore and George W. Bush.

The good news is, the election is nearing a conclusion. Al Gore has indicated that, if he loses the next round of arguments at the Florida Supreme Court, and if the Seminole and Martin county cases do not give him the presidency, he will consider making his legal challenge of the 2000 election a mere "hobby" while he applies for professorships at various universities.

Gore says he believes he still has a 50–50 chance of prevailing, though some observers contend that Kato Kaelin has a greater likelihood of being named the head of NASA. Nonetheless, it's easy to understand why Gore is fighting so hard. As he says repeatedly, fairness requires that not merely *some* of the votes, but *all* the votes in Democratic strongholds be counted. He knows that, according to analyses of the Florida vote by the *Orlando Sentinel* and the *Miami Herald,* he really did win the election, and that it was merely an oversight on the part of the Framers that the Constitution makes no mention of the *Orlando Sentinel* or the *Miami Herald.*

Gore's lead lawyer, David Boies, assures Gore that he can win this case in the courts. Boies points out that he recently persuaded a federal judge to break up America's most successful technology company on the grounds that there weren't enough other companies making money in the technology industry. Boies says his life's dream is to persuade a judge that cows in pastures are secretly plotting to take over the government.

The vice president still faces a number of significant legal and political obstacles:

- When Gore contested the election, a judge ruled against him on every count, plus some additional counts that no one had brought up, and said that, if it were up to him, Gore would be imprisoned and tried for treason.
- The U.S. Supreme Court, in its per curiam order, said that it would get "huffibrium" (huffy) if the Florida Supreme Court tries any more "humericus gobitatus" (funny stuff).
- And finally, Democrats in Congress, alarmed by Gore's stubbornness, say that if he continues to fight even after a loss at the Florida Supreme Court they will be forced to stage an interven-

tion. They will explain to Gore that his belief that he may yet become president is something that happens to *everyone* who wins the popular vote yet somehow loses the electoral college because of a tiny handful of citizens who can't correctly punch a ballot, and that the medications that treat this disorder have few permanent side effects.

George W. Bush, meanwhile, is feeling confident at the latest turn of events. Bush does not yet want to be called the "president-elect," but he has suggested that Gore be called the "vice president–reject." Bush is moving rapidly ahead in his transition, and plans to learn this week what the different cabinet positions are, and which ones are the most important.

On Tuesday, Bush received his first "intelligence briefing." Officials said the procedure did not appear to be working, and they will now consider a direct surgical implant.

Dec. 8, 12:42 P.M.

Over the past month a lot of my e-mail has arrived in Caps Lock mode. This is one of the side effects of the amazing presidential election. A typical message says something like HEY IDIOT HOW DO YOU GET PAID FOR WRITING THAT STINKING GUANO I BET YOUR PARENTS ARE ASHAMED PLEASE SHUT UP MORON BYE.

Others are even more personal, along the lines of DUMB HAIRCUT. YOU LOOK LIKE DOG BARF.

Still others start out gently.

"I consider myself a rational person of even temperament," a message will say in an extremely ominous opening. "Nonetheless I believe that your most recent column is the most contemptible piece of writing I have encountered since *Mein Kampf . . .*"

What's really upsetting to me is that these messages are from my own editor. The e-mails from *outside* the building have been too profane to quote in this family-friendly medium.

This election has infuriated a great many otherwise even-keeled people. Hotheads are all over TV and the radio. On the op-ed page, normally contemplative pundits have been squealing like a dentist's drill. To listen to these folks, you'd think our nation was at grave risk, that there are all these conscienceless monsters roaming around out there trying to subvert our democracy. Both sides think the other has tried to steal an election.

The truth is, no one tried to steal anything. Al Gore and George W. Bush both had plausible claims to victory. (I shift to past tense because, as I write, the judicial rulings are about to come out. You can sense a Gore loss the way you can tell it's about to snow.) The Florida mess was created by what was essentially a statistical fluke, the fact that Bush's margin of victory was so ridiculously small. Suddenly all the quirks and mistakes and shenanigans of Election Day came into play. Gore had a right to contest the vote— exit polls showing Gore beating Bush may have accurately reflected voter intention.

The biggest crimes in the past month have been the accusations themselves—the cheap shots from partisans. Republicans and Democrats have impugned the integrity of one another at every opportunity. Republicans predicted that Democratic judges and Democrat-controlled canvassing boards would manufacture enough votes for the vice president to hand him a victory. Guess what: They didn't.

The dirty little secret of this case is that there aren't very many dirty little secrets. Essentially the entire drama has been played out in the open—in the "sunshine," as they say in Florida. We've been able to observe the legal skirmishing on live television. A high point was the Supreme Court hearing last week, when we heard what an oral argument before the nation's highest court sounds like.

In Florida we saw some top-shelf lawyering. Barry Richard, who looks like a schoolmaster from a Dickens novel—he is not someone from whom you would want to request a second helping of gruel—was razor-sharp, tireless, and always perfectly coiffed.

David Boies, who one reader said looked like Peter Boyle playing a homeless man, was ready for every question hurled his way. His tone was: I'm so glad you asked that. My tripartite answer is as follows . . .

Boies, unfortunately, had a dog of a case. What Gore wanted—selective cleansing of the data—struck too many people as fundamentally unfair. Several of the Florida justices alluded to the problem: How, they said, can you do a recount in just a few counties, and not all of them?

Boies tried to wriggle out of it. He said, "There's never been a rule that says you have to recount all the ballots in an election contest." There's no rule, true—but this is an odd moment to be arguing the need to stick to technicalities, since, technically, Gore lost about four times already.

It's true that the law doesn't require a statewide recount. But fairness would. Bush, of course, vigorously opposed a recount—winners never ask for another chance to tally the score—but Gore should have pushed for it, hard, from the very start. He should not have tried to cherry-pick in South Florida.

Kids, take this lesson home: There are moments when you shouldn't listen to your lawyer. Don't ask what the statutes permit. Don't ask how you can take advantage of the rules. Ask what's fair.

Of course, it was easy for me, sitting in my pod, to tell the Gore team what it should have done in the first days after the election. The situation on the ground in Florida had been more complicated and confusing. Discretion for conducting recounts was given to the individual county canvassing boards. A request for a recount has to be made within seventy-two hours of an election. Gore's people, parachuting into the state, would have had to high-tail it to sixty-seven different counties and ask for recounts. In some of those places they don't care for Democrats, much less northern lawyers.

In any case, this was the day—December 8—that the election was supposed to end. The Florida Supreme Court would issue its decision. I spent some of the afternoon wandering the street, imagining life after the Recount, remembering what it was like when you had to search to find the story of the day. When I returned to the newsroom people were moving quickly—the body language of urgent news. By a 4–3 vote the Florida Supreme Court, with Chief Judge Charles Wells dissenting (and warning of a "constitutional crisis"), had ordered a full manual recount of "undervote" ballots to start immediately—throughout the state. Suddenly it appeared that Gore might actually pull out the most improbable of last-minute victories. The Bush team immediately appealed the ruling to the U.S. Supreme Court. My morning spew was suddenly out of date. I needed to produce some emergency afternoon spew. It didn't have to be good, it just had to be fast.

Dec. 8, 5:31 P.M.

Constitutional crisis! Bedlam in the nation's capital! Ladies and gentlemen, the 2000 presidential campaign IS JUST GETTING STARTED.

This is the campaign that cannot be killed. You can stab it in the heart. You can cut off its head. You can burn it and bury it. But it will not die. The campaign is stronger than all of us. It may soon begin to spread to other inhabited planets in the galaxy.

Today's shocking Florida Supreme Court ruling, funded by the Cable TV Talking Head Full Employment Act, raises the possibility that we will not know who the next president will be until the actual swearing-in ceremony on Inauguration Day. Indeed, there could be dueling ceremonies, dueling inaugurations, dueling parades. When Al Gore and George W. Bush see the presidential limo they will both lunge for it. Bush, I predict, will be the first to shout "Shotgun!"

Gore's hopes had dimmed dramatically all week. It had to be a blow to Gore when Joe Lieberman endorsed Bush. Polls showed that 60 percent believed that the vice president should concede, and this just among the members of his immediate family. Gore, however, showed resolve and let Americans understand that he has stocked the basement of the vice president's mansion with a four-year supply of dried beans, rice, and canned meat.

Earlier today, two circuit court judges ruled against Gore, and thousands of political journalists immediately began booking flights to vacation spots in the Caribbean. Then came the Florida Supreme Court ruling, which, tipping its hand right in the first paragraph, said, "Let's get nasty."

The court was quite devilish: It said it agreed with Bush. A hand recount in just a few South Florida counties would be unfair, it said. So let's do a hand recount everywhere! We'll show you what "fair" is!

Gore was fond of saying during the past year that "it's still early." Meaning, millions of Americans just hadn't gotten around to paying attention to the presidential campaign and noticing what a swell candidate he was. Gore took forever to get hot. He finally began closing the gap with George W. Bush in the last few days before the election. Gore campaigned like a madman right up to November 7, and at midnight was down in Florida, asking for votes . . . and at 1:00 A.M. . . . 2:00 A.M. . . . 3:00 A.M. . . . Still campaigning away at four in the morning.

He didn't quit. He still hasn't. This is the campaign that couldn't find its own exit strategy. The last line of the story is the same as it's been all along:

To be continued . . .

Gore's resurrection lasted less than twenty-four hours. Saturday afternoon the U.S. Supreme Court ruled 5–4 to stop the recount. Justice Scalia tipped the court's hand: There was a strong likelihood, he wrote, that Bush would prevail in his appeal. The court scheduled oral arguments for Monday morning. I went to the Supreme Court again, trolled for quotes, then rushed back and wrote a column while we waited for the networks to play a tape of the hearing. I was hoping to produce something that would remain up-to-date and publishable for at least two or three hours.

Dec. 11, 12:42 P.M.

We knew on Election Day that it was going to be close. Then the numbers came in. It was unbelievably close. It was down to Florida, and George W. Bush had a lead that kept shrinking. Bush by fifty thousand. . . . Bush by twenty-thousand . . . Bush by less than two thousand. Eventually it was Bush by three hundred, and then, Friday afternoon, by order of the Florida Supreme Court, it was Bush by 154.

Now, finally, the election is at the U.S. Supreme Court, where it appears the final margin will be Bush by one.

As I write, the attorneys are presenting their arguments. The legal experts say Gore can prevail only if his attorneys can win over one of the two swing justices, Sandra Day O'Connor or Anthony Kennedy. The first words out of David Boies's mouth will undoubtedly be something along the lines of, "Justices, I love what you've done with your hair."

The situation outside the Supreme Court this morning looked like something from the fall of communist Eastern Europe, one of those Prague or Bucharest scenes, with throngs of people in heavy coats assembling under a gray sky to protest in favor of democracy. There are two sides to this protest, with two definitions of democracy. Not even a Supreme Court ruling is going to change anyone's mind at this point.

A man carried a sign saying, "Look Out Al! Here Comes the Controlling Legal Authority!" In the middle of the sign was a picture of Justice Antonin Scalia.

Along came a lawyer for the Gore team, Neal Katyal. He carried a yellow legal pad, pressing it closely to his chest as one might a good poker hand. Was he optimistic? "Quite," he said. "If you read the submissions filed yesterday, the arguments Bush advanced read like a committee document. The arguments contradict one another." He said this while weaving through the Bush and Gore protesters, who were themselves quite busy contradicting one another.

A couple of screamers faced off in front of the cameras:

"Count them!" shouted the Gore supporter.

"Why are Democrats always victims? Why are Democrats always victims?" said the Bush man.

"What are you afraid of?"

"You lost, accept it!"

"Just count the votes! We'll all take *one* count!"

"They have already been counted!"

Jesse Jackson showed up, to no one's surprise. He described the case as a civil rights struggle. "In modern history it ranks with the challenge in Birmingham for public accomodations, in Selma for the right to vote," Jackson said as he searched for the court entrance. "In court terms, it ranks with Dred Scott. Eighty percent of those disenfranchised in Florida are African-Americans, plus the Holocaust survivors in West Palm Beach. It ranks with *Plessy v. Ferguson.*"

Senator Orrin Hatch rolled up, with a thoroughly different view.

"It's clear that at least five justices are concerned about standardless ballot counts," Hatch said. "You can't change the rules after the election."

When Representative Henry Hyde, the great impeacher, arrived, I asked him how it could be that two historically rare events, an impeachment and an election decided in the courts, could have happened within two years of each other.

"It's the Age of Aquarius!" he said.

At this highest of high courts, the presidential election may actually be ending. We have heard it said that the U.S. Supreme Court should avoid a split decision. But that would also be the most appropriate outcome. Only a narrow 5–4 split along ideological lines would suitably record for posterity the closeness and craziness of this election.

We need a majority opinion with concurring opinions all over the map, some truly incomprehensible reasoning, the logic as inscrutable as ancient hieroglyphics. We need blatant hypocrisy and transparent partisan maneuvering. We need justices to repudiate shamelessly all their previous beliefs on judicial activism and states' rights.

The perfect result? A majority opinion that no one can understand. A document banged out in a hurry, laced with typographical errors and demonstrably incorrect citations and at least one inadvertent transposition of the names Bush and Gore.

Then the Court can hurriedly issue a corrected opinion titled "What We Meant to Say."

My morning column seemed ancient by mid-afternoon. Back to the keyboard.

Dec. 11, 5:56 P.M.

The following transcript of internal Supreme Court deliberations is of unknown provenance and its authenticity has not yet been confirmed.

REHNQUIST: All right everybody, we've obviously got a fine mess on our hands. Who wants to start?

STEVENS: Well, it's clear that Snyder was rash to fire Norv before the end of the season. To lose to Dallas is simply—

REHNQUIST: Not the Redskins. Bush and Gore. Florida. Presidential race. We're supposed to somehow solve this damn thing . . .

KENNEDY: Where's the federal question here? How do we even know we have jurisdiction?

SCALIA: Tony, we're the U.S. [expletive] Supreme [expletive]

Court. Emphasis on the "Supreme." We can do anything we want. We can make Nader the winner if we find that outcome to be sufficiently amusing.

THOMAS: Ditto. Whatever Nino says.

BREYER: We should have interrupted more today. Especially when that doofus Klock was up there calling people by their wrong names.

REHNQUIST: What we can't do is simply remand this to the Florida court. Last time we did that they ignored us. They acted like we didn't exist. I think it's time we gave these crackers a jurisprudential wedgie they'll never forget.

O'CONNOR: Oh, heavens to Betsy, this is all so crazy. We don't normally tell state courts what to do. Not that I want to rule in favor of Gore, who I find very unappealing, but I just don't know if that Florida ruling is really that awful.

KENNEDY: You thinking about swinging, Sandy? We could swing together.

O'CONNOR: You devil.

SOUTER: I think there are serious equal protection issues we should consider. Remember when I asked Boies how we should instruct the Florida courts on ballot standards? And he had brain lock for about five seconds? And then finally could only say, "That's a very difficult question"? Well, obviously this is the weak link for the Gore people. They know they can only win if we allow them to count dimpled, pregnant, slightly poofed-in chads. They know that they got those votes in Broward on ballots where the chads were just sort of theoretically indented. If we apply a rigorous standard then they'll lose the Broward votes and won't win the recount. Isn't that clever that I figured that out?

SCALIA: My IQ is immeasurably greater than yours, David. Why can't you ever admit it? I can recite *Marbury v. Madison* from memory, including footnotes.

GINSBURG: Let me get one thing straight. The Bush people say that there is a vague standard for examining ballots in Florida, that the standard speaks only of "the will of the voter." What one county considers a vote might not pass muster in another county. But who created this vague standard? Not the Florida Supreme Court. The legislature wrote the standard. So why are we trying to punish the Florida Supreme Court for simply asking that the votes be counted according to how the legislature defined a vote?

STEVENS: Also the punt coverage is abysmal.

SCALIA: Ruth, I think you don't quite grasp the big picture here, as I do so easily with my basketball-sized brain. This is the month of December. Elections are held the first Tuesday in November. The election is over. The votes were counted, then recounted according to a statutory process. Gore got some fancy lawyers to contest the election and now it's a free-for-all down there. We don't have any assurance that there aren't hijinks being perpetrated; there's no time for further legal challenges should there be fraud; the whole process is arbitrary; and at some point we have to say, "no more."

THOMAS: Mega-dittos.

REHNQUIST: I love the part where I pound the gavel and say, "The case is submitted." You know I practice that at home.

On December 12, the bitterly divided United States Supreme Court ruled 5–4 in favor of Bush. The majority, comprised of conservatives appointed by Republican presidents, argued that the different standards used in the recounts represented a violation of the equal protection clause of the Constitution. The decision would be enormously controversial, but it didn't matter. There was no higher court.

Dec. 13

The following is a draft of the Supreme Court decision in *Bush v. Gore*, discovered in a dumpster on Capitol Hill.

PER CURIAM

In keeping with the Court's ambition to provide an unambiguous and unanimous decision in *Bush v. Gore*, and thereby legitimate the outcome of the 2000 presidential election, we present herein a majority opinion signed by Justices Rehnquist, Scalia, Thomas, O'Connor, and Kennedy, with a partial dissent to the majority by Justices Rehnquist, Scalia, and Thomas, a full dissent by Justices Stevens, Souter, Breyer, and Ginsburg, a partial dissent to the full dissent by Justices Breyer and Souter, a needling, invective-filled dissent to the partial dissent to the majority opinion from Scalia, a spitwad [attached] from Justice Stevens and a chunk of hair [attached] ripped from the head of Justice Kennedy by Justice Ginsburg during final deliberations.

The Court will note that it did manage on Tuesday afternoon to assemble a respectable 6–3 majority in favor of the Chinese takeout.

This Court acknowledges that, under the Constitution, a presidential election is truly a series of state elections, all procedures of which are presumed governed by state legislators and judges. We hereby void that presumption in states whose configuration can be described as "peninsular."

This ruling, though admittedly unusual, is grounded in our belief that Florida is a rogue state whose judicial apparatus is facially null per 3 USC Section 5 Chapter 11 Verse 21 Footnote 8. None of the justices in the majority have actually read that clause recently but we vaguely recall it from law school.

The accounting of an election must submit to the conjoined priorities of accuracy and finality. Obviously this election will achieve neither. No one will ever know the "real" vote, and this will continue to be a subject of fierce argument even as the sun begins to cool and gradually expand and turn into what astronomers refer to as a red giant. We encourage the public to avoid conspiracy theories, and hereby reject the suggestion in the Gore brief that, if you examine the Zapruder film closely, it appears that James A. Baker is the "umbrella man."

Deadlines in elections must be respected. There is clearly not enough time to complete the recount of ballots in Florida, expose that recount to legal challenge and judicial review, and remain faithful to the December 12 "Safe Harbor" provision under which electors cannot be challenged in Congress. In retrospect it might be argued that this Court did not speed up the process by halting the vote count on Saturday: Castigating public officials for taking too long in a process that we have stopped altogether is something this Court finds amusing.

Moreover, this Court is extremely concerned that the Florida election has resulted in violence to the equal protection clause—specifically, the recount is unfair to those voters whose unfair advantage had already been in place before the election. We stipulate that, speaking very generally, affluent citizens in precincts using optical-scanning equipment enjoy a significant advantage over the votes of poor and minority citizens in precincts using antiquated punch card balloting. On the other hand, the Framers didn't think that blacks and women and poor people should be allowed to vote, period. Let's keep this in perspective.

We confess that it requires a certain intellectual finesse to declare that the real victims in the Florida recount were the Bush voters, but we will remind the public that we have lifetime appointments and cannot be fired. At times, we feel like gods. Chief Justice Rehnquist can report with authority that there is no greater pleasure in life than killing ants in one's kitchen with a Supreme Court gavel.

Inevitably, this ruling will be criticized as "political." Cynics, unfamiliar with the historic independence of the nation's highest court, will point out that the majority is comprised entirely of justices appointed by Republican presidents, and that two of the justices in the majority were explicitly criticized during the campaign by the vice president. This ruling, however, is not the slightest bit political. It's personal.

Several of us on this court are desperate to retire. We don't want some liberal Democrat to appoint our successor. If Bush becomes president, for example, Justice O'Connor can step down and spend the spring playing tennis in Scottsdale. She is reputed to be unforgiving and obstinate in her line calls. Justice Rehnquist will also retire, and Justice Scalia will be appointed the chief justice, from which perch he can rain terror upon the sodomites and connivers and mushy-brained liberals who have brought this once great nation to the edge of ruin.

Let us finally address the defendant directly. Mr. Vice President, we have you surrounded. Come out with your hands up. You will not be harmed. You still have a great future ahead of you. Think of your family.

It is so ordered.

Dec. 14

So dies the Election from the Black Lagoon. It was horrible and fabulous at the same time. It is statistically improbable that we will see such a thing again in our lifetimes.

Now we must turn our attention to cabinet appointments, snowstorms, and meetings of the board of governors of the Federal Reserve. While we weren't looking, America apparently was plunged into a recession. We will find out in a few days if Alan Greenspan supports lower interest ratesZZZZZZZZZZZZZZ.

This is a time for graciousness, for healing, for unity. This is a time to end the invective and hostility, to join together as a people with common values and a shared destiny. (I will go on vacation until this unendurable period comes to an end.)

The Florida recount was a fine little war, vigorously prosecuted on multiple fronts, with unexpected heroes and villains and absolutely nothing obvious about its outcome. As mega-stories go, the recount was more edifying than Impeachment, and not so fundamentally tragic and grotesque as the O.J. trial. It's hard to think of a story that so thoroughly captured the nation's attention that did not involve sex or death.

It is surely not a trivial matter that, when the ballots were fed into the machines on the night of the election, Bush got more votes. In the automatic recount he still had more votes. From that point on, both sides waged their battle within the confines of the law. The law itself was the problem: It was gaseous at the core. It had no clear standard for determining the legitimacy of a vote. After all the legal warfare and judicial rulings, there's still not a clear standard for determining "the intent of the voter."

The Gore partisans think Bush staged a coup with the help of conservatives on the U.S. Supreme Court and Jeb Bush's political machine in Florida. But there aren't enough hard facts to support so alarming a thesis. There are many troubling elements to this tale, from the TV network blunders on election night to the startling number of "spoiled" ballots in some predominantly African-American precincts. It's disturbing that so many partisan hacks got involved in the process of determining what would be a fair outcome. That said, any way you tabulate the results in Florida, you still wind up with what amounts to a statistical tie. Neither candidate really "won" Florida.

The election was an improbable event, an unnatural disaster, one for which we had inadequate emergency procedures. This was an asteroid striking the earth. Florida was the impact crater.

For all the rage and craziness of the thirty-six-day Election Night, we can still take a smidgen of pride in the way we transfer presidential power. So perhaps it wasn't the smoothest handoff we've ever seen. We'll stipulate that it required most of the lawyers currently practicing in the United States. We'll note that the prospect of having the nation's future decided by officials in Florida was roughly as reassuring as being told that, although the airplane's pilot and co-pilot are dead, the flight attendant at the controls has extensive experience with a Game Boy.

We'll acknowledge that the final Supreme Court ruling was something of a dog's breakfast, not the kind of thing you really want to look at too closely.

Still, the battle ended beautifully. Al Gore and George W. Bush last night made perfect speeches. They were liberated by the resolution of the election. For a moment it didn't feel like a bitter end after all.

There are countries where the transfer of power involves no lawyers, because it involves no laws. The army just takes care of the whole thing. One day your president vanishes, replaced by the new maximum leader, a general with a giant torso, a square head, tiny eyes, and a reputation (according to some expert from Brookings or AEI) for employing torture only when he feels it's truly necessary.

Our process may not be perfect but at least it's entirely transparent. The war was fought in our living rooms, twenty-four hours a day—there were times when you didn't dare risk turning away from the cable TV news long enough to go to the bathroom. We witnessed every strategic maneuver, read every ruling, and looked over the shoulders of officials examining ballots. In America we keep our politics on the record.

The combatants have nothing to be ashamed of. They did what they had to do. Gore should go mend his fences, enjoy his family, write a book, and get away from the strategists and handlers and, most of all, the TV cameras and their reality-distorting lenses. He should somehow summon the strength to put another presidential run out of his mind, at least for a few months.

Forget the pundits who say Bush will take the oath of office in a weakened position. The presidency is more imperial than ever.

He runs a country that has never been richer or stronger or more influential around the world. By a margin of 537 votes, or by a margin of millions—it doesn't really matter—George W. Bush is now the most powerful man on the planet.

Except, of course (I just can't help it), for Dick Cheney.

EPILOGUE

Saturday, January 20, 2001

It was a challenging inauguration. The weather was vile. The rain came just in time for Thursday's opening ceremonies, and lingered, not even a real rain but a kind of indeterminate drizzle, cold, unforgiving, the kind that not even the thickest fox, mink, or rabbit fur can repel. A chill wind blew from the west. Then came the plague of toads. Thousands fled in terror as a swarm of locusts moved in from the south. I've covered every inauguration since Harding's, and this is the first time I've seen fissures open up in the crust of the Earth. When the puddles of water turned to blood I'm sure many Americans began to wonder if this was some kind of "sign" from above. Please, in the spirit of harmony, let's not jump to conclusions.

Thousands of people showed up for the inauguration with the firmest of convictions that George W. Bush is a fraud, that his claim to power is illegitimate. Among these cynics, only Al Gore held his tongue. He declined to exercise his Constitutional and moral right to heckle Bush unmercifully throughout the inaugural address. Many of us expected Gore to whip out some papers and shout, "Late results from Broward County!"

I chose to watch the first part of the ceremony on the streets, among the people, the common folk, the citizens, the *Vulgus,* to experience the inauguration in its most authentic and populist form. Mine was a distant vantage point. Indeed, I may have actually been in Arlington. If I squinted really hard, I could see, far in the distance, a tiny object that I am pretty sure was the Capitol dome.

All around me were the protesters. Throughout Campaign 2000 they'd been at the major events, angry, declaring the process a fraud, denouncing the dark forces that put profits over people. They'd suspected that the system was rigged from the get-go; the recount had been the final piece of confirmation.

"Unity my Ashcroft!" one sign said.

"Re-elect Gore in 2004."

"Dubya: Buffoon King of Corporate Whores, Earth Plunderers, and Election Thieves."

"It's a sad day, because democracy was subverted," said Connie Anguili, a protester from the District.

"Nobody cares about democracy as long as there's a smooth transition of power," said her friend Arlene Whitten.

"I really would like somebody who's actually been elected," Anguili said.

"Not by Supreme Court corruption," added Whitten.

The new president spoke of unity, common ideals, shared values, but the protesters had long since tuned him out. They had no interest in his speech—I didn't see anyone even carrying a radio to catch what the evil man was saying. For them, the theft of the presidency has become as fixed and immutable a chapter of American history as the French and Indian War.

I caught a glimpse of Bush on Friday night at the overhyped and underfunned Black Tie and Boots ball at the Marriott Wardman. It was a Texas gig, complete with the big hair crowd and a miniature oil derrick in the lobby (just what Washington needs, more of that "Houston" feeling). Bush seemed to be having a good time. He was chuckling, strutting, and crafting really short sentences. The natural length of an unscripted George W. Bush sentence is somewhere in the vicinity of five words. Some are three words, some four, and he can go double-digits if you plant a comma in the middle. Be generous: It's not a mental deficiency, it's a style, just like it's his style to cry, to be a "weeper," as he put it. He communicates emotionally, not informationally. Say good-bye to a president who cites endless statistics; say hi to a guy who loves ya.

"I love you!" he told his fellow Texans. "And I love Texas! And I love my wife, the next first lady! She lookin' good, isn't she? Pretty good for Midland, Texas."

He looked fit and tanned, strikingly boyish for someone in his fifties. He was wearing his imminent responsibility lightly. Walking across the confetti-littered floor, I found myself having serious "meaning" problems, struggling with the sense that vapidity had triumphed, that it would be a long four years. This inaugural weekend was turning out to be very much like a political convention, only without the *substance*.

The inauguration itself nearly redeemed everything that had come before. The scene on the stage on the west side of the Capitol was startling to behold after so many months of bitterness: The partisans of the vicious battle in Florida were suddenly shoulder to shoulder. There was former President Bush and his wife Barbara, watching their son take the oath. A few feet away sat Jimmy and Rosalynn Carter. Colin Powell. The Supreme Court justices. Senators from both parties. Jim Baker. Coretta Scott King.

The Clintons and the Gores.

A soldier came forth and sang the national anthem. For a few moments all the issues and arguments receded.

What was Bush thinking? It was impossible to know, but he had a gravity that had been missing at the party the night before. He looked confident, in control, ready for the job. He gave a good speech, somber, religious, with a final flourish about an angel in a whirlwind. He didn't do anything to ruin the occasion, such as offering the Chief Justice a big wad of cash in exchange for the presidency.

As for Al Gore, he was silent, of course. He had no official role to play on this day, other than that of observer. It was his nature and his duty to be gracious. He sat there inertly, enduring the cold, the drizzle, and the speech of the man that he'd beaten nationally by—the final numbers had come in—539,898 votes.

But who's counting?

INDEX

LINKS AND ACKNOWLEDGMENTS

You can find information about registering to vote at http://www.fee.gov/votregis/vr.htm.

The official returns of the 2000 election, state by state, can be found at http://fecwebl.fec.gov/pubrec/2000presgeresults.htm.

To read the latest "Rough Draft" column or peruse its archive, go to http://washingtonpost.com/wp-dyn/nation/columns/roughdraft/.

To read the *Washington Post*'s multipart chronicle of the Florida recount, go to http://washingtonpost.com/wp-dyn/articles/A54719-2001Jan27.html.

If that's too complicated, go to washingtonpost.com and find the On Politics channel.

To read an excerpt of the author's previous book, *Captured by Aliens,* go to http://www.simonandschuster.com/excerpt.cfm?isbn-0684848562.

Readers can contact the author at achenbachj@washpost.com. Enraged, semicoherent diatribes about liberal whiners should be directed to rush@eibnet.com.

There are writers who do not need editors, and I'm not one of them. (Does that sentence make any sense? I can never tell!) My profuse thanks to Tracy Grant and Mary Hadar for greatly improving this material on deadline and tending to my delicate psyche with the care normally afforded certain frost-sensitive tropical plants.

Alice Mayhew miraculously turned the material into a book and got it published almost before I finished typing the last page.

Many thanks to: Kevin Achenbach, Chuck Babington, Mike Baker, Dan Balz, Dave Barry, David Broder, Craig Cola, Steve Coll, Len Downie, Doug Feaver, David Finkel, Marc Fisher, Robin Groom, John Harris, Jonathan Jao, Roger Labrie, David Maraniss, Lynn Medford, Kevin Merida, Ellen Nakashima, Jim and Emily Notestein, Mark Patterson, Gene Robinson, David Rosenthal, Anja Schmidt, Chris Schroeder, Tom Shroder, Mark Stencel, Lisa Todorovich, Lexie Verdon, David Von Drehle, and Gene Weingarten.

Michael Congdon provided invaluable editorial guidance, in addition to doing everything else that agents do.

And Mary Stapp made everything better.